the Stars

by

E. RAYMOND CAPT M.A., A.I.A., F.S.A. Scot.

Archaeological Institute of America

with

COVER DESIGN AND ORIGINAL ILLUSTRATIONS BY J.A. DRYBURGH

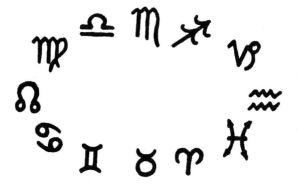

PUBLISHER
ARTISAN PUBLISHERS
P.O. Box 1529
Muskogee, Oklahoma 74402
(918) 682-8341
www.artisanpublishers.com

ISBN 0-934666-02-4
Library of Congress catalog card number: 79-116390

1

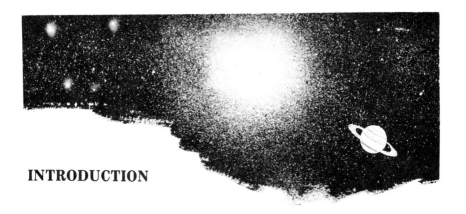

INTRODUCTION

Gazing upon the multitude of stars that shine in the nocturnal heavens, one might despair of reading anything intelligible in their design - they seem to be so scattered, so entirely without order, spread with such confusion over the face of the sky.

As we behold these twinkling points of light, shining down from their serene heights, we recall the words of the Psalmist.

"The heavens declare the glory of God and the firmament sheweth his handiwork. Day unto day uttereth speech, and night unto night sheweth knowledge...Their line is gone out through all the earth, and their words to the end of the world. In them hath he set a tabernacle for the sun" (Psalm 19: 1-4).

Having declared that the heavens reveal God's glory, the Psalmist informs us that the heavens declare a message in a language that is understood by all peoples. These starry worlds, as such, do show forth His *"handiwork"*, but explain little about the *"glory of God"*. How then can the stars be made to speak, in a language everyone can understand?

The answer is quite evident. Pictures speak in all dialects. They speak a universal language, to all peoples everywhere. Somewhere in the earliest ages of human existence the visible stars were named. Certain ones were arranged into groups by someone thoroughly familiar with the laws of astronomy. Those names and groupings were at the same time included in certain figures, natural or imaginary, but intensely symbolic and significant. Today we know them as the Constellations.

Twelve constellations make up the Zodiac. These major stargroupings form a belt which circles the sky close to the plane of the earth's orbit around the sun. Modern atlases list them in the following order: Aries, Taurus, Gemini, Cancer, Leo, Virgo, Libra, Scorpio, Sagittarius, Capricorn, Aquarius and Pisces.

It is well known that the ancient races drew charts of these Zodiacal Signs; that ancient astrology was actually the father of astronomy. Astronomers sometimes denounce the Zodiac as unnatural and confusing, yet they have never been able to brush it aside or to substitute anything better or more convenient in its place. The Signs of the Zodiac are part of the common universal language of astronomical science.

The Zodiac is found in religious faiths and pagan superstitions. Astrology is based upon it. The Bible is replete with it. The Companion Bible tells us that all the verbs in the second half of Psalm 19 are of an astronomical nature. The written words of Scripture parallel the words written in the heavens and preserved in the Signs of the Zodiac.

Authors of books on astronomy, when referring to the figures associated with the constellations, speak of the antiquity of their origin. Without exception they are unable to give the source of the inspiration which resulted in the naming and meaning of the pictorial groupings. The existence of Zodiacal figures have been traced in all ages and among all nations, with all their features settled and fixed from the most distant periods. Learned antiquarians of modern times have searched every page of heathen mythology, ransacked all the legends of poetry and fables to answer the question, Who framed this system? Investigations of all the religions, sciences, customs and traditions of every nation, tribe and people have failed to discover who first so accurately observed the celestial bodies and so sublimely wove them together into one great scheme. What the stars were meant to signify, over and above what is evidenced by their own nature, interpreters have been at a loss to tell us.

Were such wonderful creations of almighty power and wisdom without purpose or meaning? Was there some original, divine science connected with the star designs? Is there evidence to show it was the will of the Eternal God and that His sons and daughters enjoy His handiwork and understand His glory?

The purpose of this study is to present the findings of past eminent scholars, together with those of modern scientific investigators, in order to show the stars do reveal *"words written in the heavens"* - words that declare the *"glory of God"*.

THE STARS

The stars are suns, heavenly bodies shining by their own light and generally so far away from us that, moving rapidly, they seem fixed in their position. Although several thousand stars are visible on the clearest night, a telescope reveals multitudes more. The total in our universe may run into billions, but even so, space is almost empty. The nearest star, our sun, is a mere 93 million miles away. The next nearest star is 26 million-million miles distant, nearly 300,000 times farther than our sun.

The stars that are visible to the naked eye are divided into six magnitudes, or orders of brightness. But these are arbitrary, and the actual graduations are innumerable. In fact it would be difficult to find two stars, ranked as first magnitude, of equal brightness. The inequality in some cases is very great; "for one star differeth from another star in glory". There are 21 stars classified as of the first magnitude, or highest degree of brightness. These are scattered over the heavens and have their own individual names. The fourteen brightest stars in the order of their brightness are as follows:

Name	Apparent Magnitude	Distance in Light-years	Spectral Type
Sirius	−1.58	9	A0
Canopus	−0.86	650?	F0
Alpha Centauri	0.06	4	G0, K5
Vega	0.14	26	A0
Capella	0.21	47	G0
Arcturus	0.24	41	K0
Rigel	0.34	540?	B8
Procyon	0.48	10	F5
Achernar	0.60	66	B5
Beta Centauri	0.86	300	B1
Altair	0.89	16	A5
Betelgeuse	0.92v.	190	M0
Alpha Crucis	1.05	230	B1
Aldebaran	1.06	57	K5

The star Canopus is much farther away from us than is Sirius. In reality it is estimated to be many times brighter than Sirius, radiating many times the heat and light. Vega is one of the very bright suns of the universe and is 50 times brighter than our sun. The stars differ - not only in brightness but also in color. Even those that are called white, show surprising chromatic variation. Both Sirius and Vega are classified as white, but the former has a shade of green and the latter a distinct tinge of blue. Capella is creamy white. Other stars vary in color. They are red, or ruddy, light rose, yellow, greenish and topaz-hued.

Nearly all the brighter stars have individual names whose meanings describe some characteristic of the star. Sometimes the name indicates the position in the constellation to which they belong. Modern astronomers designate some of the stars by Greek and Latin letters with the name of the constellation in which they are found. Many of the stars, however, retain their earlier Arabic or Hebrew names, having highly symbolic meanings.

Intense observation of the starry heavens will show that some stars hold their places from age to age. Their variations are slight, so as to be scarcely observable in thousands of years. Others are "wandering stars", changing places continually, going and returning at regular intervals. Some of them are nestled together in particular groups. Some stand alone, so as to be easily distinguished.

The sun, moon and stars rise in the east, move across the sky and set in the west. This journey is repeated day by day. One star, the "Pole Star" in the northern sky, never seems to move at all. This is the North Star, or Polaris, which happens to be on the line of the earth's axis. For centuries Polaris was used as a guide by travelers simply because of its unchanging position. Stars in its vicinity do not rise or set. They move around Polaris in circles. These circles carry them under Polaris, from west to east, and over it from east to west. Further from Polaris, the circles grow ever larger.

The most important circumpolar stars are those of the three constellations Ursa Major, Ursa Minor and Draco, with Cassiopeia and Cepheus as well. The behavior of these stars was extremely puzzling to the ancients. They could not understand why it was that one group of stars should move in a manner so different from the others, and so different from the sun and moon.

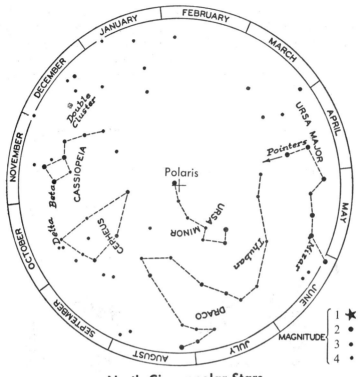

North Circumpolar Stars

It was believed by the ancient star-gazers that the north was the center of the universe, the throne from which the gods governed man and his little world. Therefore, many mythologies thought to see in the northern stars various minor divinities, powerful in their own right yet circling reverently round the throne of the supreme ruler. Such was the idea of the Greeks when they spoke of the palace of Zeus as being among the north stars. The Chinese employed the same theory when they located the throne of Shang Ti in the Pole Star. To all the ancients the stars of Ursa Major, in particular, were believed to be the nerve center from which all matters pertaining to heaven and earth were controlled.

The Pole Star, the one we call "Polaris", that appears so unchanging, has not always been the pole star nor will it continue to be. There is a shift of the Pole so slight that it cannot be observed in the space of one, or even two or three lifetimes, but in the course of as many centuries it begins to be noticeable. This is due to a gradual change in the direction of tilt of the Earth's axis because of the gravitational attraction of the Sun and Moon, which tend to pull Earth's equatorial bulge into line. This double attraction causes the Earth to wobble slightly, like a spinning top. The axis completes one rotation in about 25,800 years, which results in the exact location of the Pole to move in a slow circle around the north sky. This movement is called "the precession of the equinoxes".

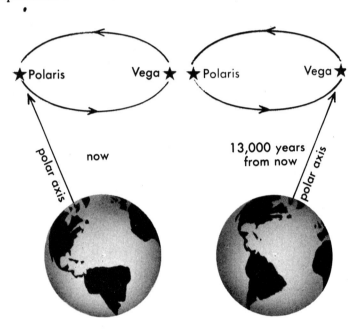

Precession

As the location of the Pole moves, different stars appear as the Pole Star. The circle shifts from Thuban, the Dragon Star which was Pole Star five thousand years ago, to our present Polaris (in the tail of Ursa Minor), then on to Alderamin in Cepheus, to Deneb, to Vega, and so back again to Thuban and Polaris. There are, of course, gaps between the various Pole Stars, long periods of time when no star is near the exact north and the stars all seem to be in motion. The whole cycle of the Pole Stars takes about 25,800 years. Polaris is a comparative newcomer to its present position. Only within the last two thousand years has it come near enough to the axis of the skies to be used in determining north. It still has some one hundred and twenty five years to go before reaching the point at which it comes nearest to the Pole. Then it will appear to us on earth as the one fixed and focal point of the heavens for many hundreds of years.

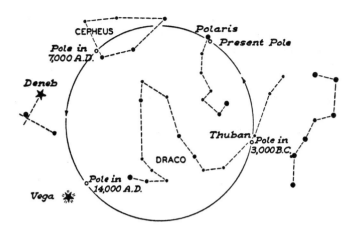

Among the circumpolar constellations is a group of seven bright stars (in Ursa Major) that form the outline of a dipper. Four of the stars form what appears to be the bowl of the dipper; the other three form its curved handle. It lies in the northern heavens and in our latitude is above the horizon all night, so that it can always be seen when the skies are clear. The two stars on the outer side of the bowl are called the "pointers" because a line drawn through them, from bottom to top, will point toward Polaris (the North Star). The line, if extended to about five times the distance between the two stars, will end approximately at Polaris.

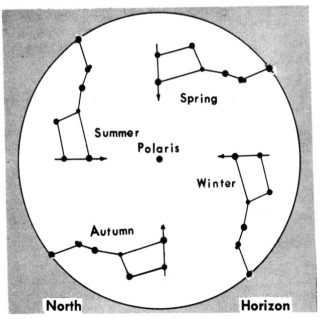

Stars of the Big Dipper move halfway around Polaris between every sunset and sunrise. However, the shape of the Dipper itself remains unaltered. To emphasize that certain stars do not change their relative positions, they are referred to as "fixed stars". Actually, however, all the stars themselves are in motion, going in various directions and at different speeds. Some stars travel alone, others in pairs. Still others travel in groups, such as the Pleiades, a cluster of stars in the constellation Taurus (the Bull).

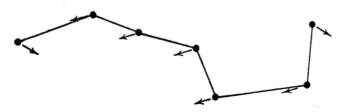

THE CHANGING FORM OF THE GREAT DIPPER

Five of the Big Dipper's stars are members of such a cluster; they are moving in the same direction through space. If all seven belonged, this group would hold together for a longer time; but there are two, the northern Pointer and the star at the end of the handle, which are preceeding in other directions. The familiar "Dipper" is going to pieces, although the change is very slow. The bent handle will bend more as time goes on and the bowl will spread. It will remain a fairly convincing dipper for twenty-five thousand years to come.

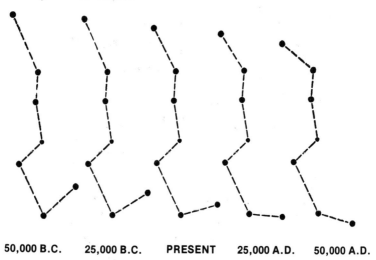

50,000 B.C.   25,000 B.C.   PRESENT   25,000 A.D.   50,000 A.D.

10

Four of our planets are often mistaken for stars. Venus and Jupiter are at certain times brighter than the brightest star. Saturn and Mars vary from second to first magnitude. To the trained observer, however, there is an unquestionable difference between the light of a planet and that of a star. The light of a planet is steadier and less affected by the phenomenon known as "scintillation" (to sparkle or twinkle). Moreover, the stars shine with a piercing light of their own while planets are dead bodies, luminated only by reflected sunlight. Altogether, there are 9 known planets in the sun's family. These planets have 31 moons, or satelites, and thousands of minor planets or "asteroids". They range in size from tiny Mercury to great Jupiter. The remaining planets are Venus, Mars, Saturn, Uranus, Neptune, Pluto and our Earth. They all move about in the heavens with seeming irregularity, but within certain limited paths. Moons revolve about all the planets except Mercury, Venus and Pluto.

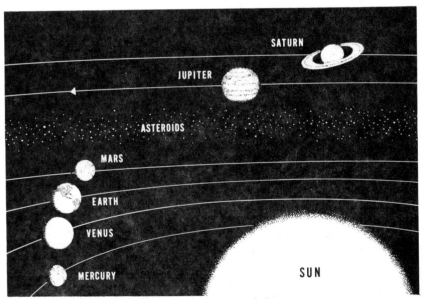

The planets move around the sun

On a clear moonless night, the Milky Way can be seen. It appears as a mysterious circle of soft, glowing light surrounding the entire firmament. The effect is caused by our looking into our "Galaxy" (a Latin name meaning milk). This is the name given to the huge star system of which the Sun and all the visible stars are a part. Our Galaxy is known as a "spiral galaxy" because it is shaped like a flattened disk with a central bulge. It has a dense nucleus

11

with less dense spiral arms winding outward. When examined through a telescope, instead of a dim glow, countless individual stars can be seen. These are as numerous as grains of sand on a beach. They are so faint and far away that the naked eye cannot distinguish them. Within our Galaxy there may be as many as 100,000 million stars and great clouds of cosmic dust (nebulae) of which new stars are constantly being formed. These rotate around the center of the Galaxy somewhat as the planets rotate around our Sun.

This greatest of all known star systems is about 100,000 light years in diameter (a light year is the distance that light, moving at the rate of 186,000 miles per second, travels in one year) and between 10,000 to 15,000 light years thick. Our Sun is close to the equatorial (long) plane of the Galaxy, but well off to one side. Our galactic center or "nucleus" appears to be about 30,000 light years away.

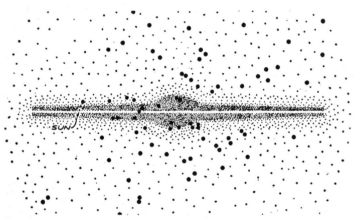

EDGEWISE VIEW OF OUR GALAXY. THE SMALL DOTS REPRESENT STARS, THE LARGER DOTS GLOBULAR STAR CLUSTERS.

There are probably a billion galaxies within the range of our 200-inch telescope, which covers a distance of 2 billion, or more, light years. They appear to be scattered at random, yet are somewhat uniformly spaced throughout the visible universe. Actually distances to far-flung galaxies are difficult, if not impossible, to determine. However, we know that our Galaxy is one of 17 galaxies spaced within 3 million light years of each other.

With this brief review of our Universe let us consider the groups of stars known as "constellations" which make up the Zodiac.

THE CONSTELLATIONS

Every atlas of the heavens is filled with figures and outlines of men, women, animals, monsters and other objects. Each one includes a certain set of stars. These figures, together with the cluster of stars they embrace, are known as "Constellations." The configurations are abstractions, bounded by certain imaginary and by no means defined lines. Some of these apparent patterns were known and used by our forefathers for thousands of years. Although it is commonly believed the characters and objects of the constellations came from Greek and Roman mythology, there is evidence of a far greater antiquity.

CELESTIAL MAP, NORTHERN HEMISPHERE, FROM A WOODCUT BY A. DURER.—ROSENWALD COLLECTION, NATIONAL GALLERY OF ART WASH. D.C.

If we examine the records of the ancient nations of the world we find the Chinese, Chaldean and Egyptian astronomers recognized the same "signs", both as to the meaning of their names and their order. This, in turn, suggests their zodiacs were but copies of an even older zodiac. Because we find such universal agreement on the constellations, it is evident that the patterns were fixed according to some well-developed religion. Sometimes the stars lend themselves naturally to the figures. In the case with Scorpio(the Scorpion), its heart is marked by the red star "Antarus", and the stars delineate a raised tail that seems ready to sting. Also it is easy to discern the horns of Taurus the Bull; the right eye being marked by a bright star called "Al Debaran". However, more often the stars suggest other, more obvious patterns. This would indicate the designer wanted the stars to conform to certain representations.

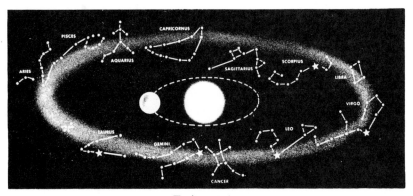

Zodiac Belt

These ancient star-pictures are in what we call the "Zodiacal Circle", an imaginary band, encircling the heavens, through which our solar system revolves. This solar path through the stars is called the "Ecliptic". The Ecliptic, if it could be viewed from immediately beneath the Polar Star, would form a complete and perfect circle, concentric with the Equator. All the stars and the sun would appear to move in this circle, never rising or setting. To a person north or south of the Equator the stars appear to rise and set obliquely, but, to a person on the Equator, they rise and set perpendicularly. Each star is twelve hours above and twelve hours below the horizon. The points where the two circles (the Ecliptic and the Equator) intersect are called the "Equinoctial Points". It is the movement of these points (which are now moving from Aries to Pisces) which gives rise to the term, "the precession of the Equinoxes" (the vast cycle of the sun).

The highest and lowest points from the celestial equator reached by the Sun as it travels along the ecliptic are called the "Solstices. The northernmost point is called "Summer Solstice (June 22; the southernmost point is called "Winter Solstice (December 22). The Summer Solstice point lies in Gemini and the Winter Solstice point lies in Sagittarius. At these points the Sun appears to stand still momentarily - hence "solstice" (solstice is Latin for "stands still").

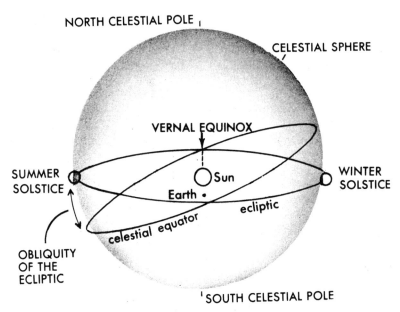

The Zodiacal Circle is divided into twelve divisions or "Signs". It is necessary to make a distinction between the "signs" of the Zodiac and the "constellations" of the Zodiac. Each sign is exactly thirty degrees long - one twelfth of the complete zone - and the first sign (Aries-in modern atlases) begins with the Vernal Equinox (about March 21, when the hours of sunlight and darkness are very nearly the same). That is, the sun always enters the sign of Aries as it passes through the Vernal Equinox. It then traverses Taurus and Gemini and enters Cancer at the Summer Solstice, after which it traverses Leo and Virgo and enters Libra as it passes through the Autumnal Equinox (about September 21, at which time the Sun crosses the celestial equator from north to south and the hours of sunlight and darkness are again nearly the same everywhere on Earth). The Sun then traverses the six signs south of the equator and enters the sign of Aries again when it arrives at the Vernal Equinox.

15

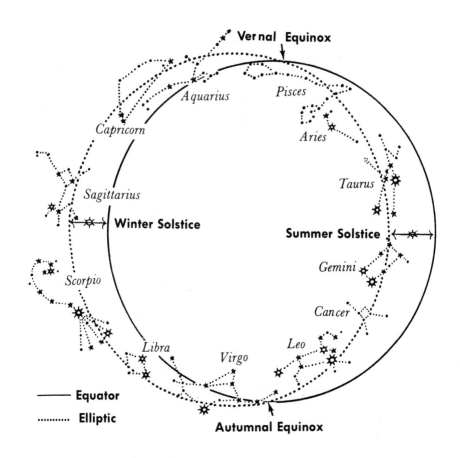

Equator

Elliptic

Equinoctial Points

The twelve groups of stars (constellations) within the boundaries of the twelve signs originally had the same names as the signs, and each constellation would remain forever within the corresponding sign if the Vernal Equinox did not move among the stars. This movement or "precession" of the equinoxes carries the signs of the Zodiac westward around the ecliptic with a constant speed that causes them to make a complete circuit of the sky in approximately 25,800 years. Thus the constellations of the Zodiac remain fixed but the signs steadily slip westward.

The sign of Aries, for the last 2000 years, has been in the Sign to the west. The signs and constellations of the Zodiac coincided about 300 B.C. and also about 26,000 B.C. The Greek writer, Hesoid, says that Arcturus, rises at sunset fifty days after the Winter Solstice. In our calendar this date would be February 19. This bright star now rises at sunset (in Greece) on March 30.

From the known rate of the shift of the constellations of the Zodiac we can determine that Hesoid lived about 2800 years ago.

We learn from the early writings of the Persians and the Chinese that there were four bright stars in the sky that protected and watched over the others. These stars were said to be in the east, the west, the north and the south. These positions evidently corresponded to the Vernal Equinox, the Autumnal Equinox, the Winter Solstice and the Summer Soltice - the four cardinal points of the sky. If we look in the vicinity of these points we can find no stars of any considerable brightness and we might be inclined to doubt the accuracy of this ancient literature or to wonder whether the four bright stars have faded considerably during the intervening years. However, when we consider the westward precession of the equinoxes, the four cardinal points would not have the same location with reference to the stars as they had ages ago, for the constellations of the Zodiac are continually slipping in an easterly direction with reference to the Vernal Equinox. We must study the Zodiac as the Persians saw it.

If we turn the Zodiac back (westward) through sixty degrees we find four bright stars, Alerbaran, Antares, Regulus and Fomalhaut, almost exactly in the places assigned to them by the Persians. Since the Zodiac has slipped through sixty degrees in about 5000 years we can tell approximately when the observations of these ancient peoples were made. It is interesting to note that the four bright stars, that the Persians and the Chinese said were in the four cardinal points of the Zodiac, are in the constellations of Taurus (the Bull), Scorpio (called by Abraham-the Eagle), Leo (the Lion) and Aquarius (the Man pouring water out of a vessel), respectively.These correspond perfectly with the four faces of the "cherubim" in the Book of Ezekiel and were the emblems of the four "brigades" (Judah, Ephraim, Reuben and Dan) of Israel in the four-square Wilderness Camp.

Ezekiel 1:10— *As for the likeness of their faces, the cherubims, they had the face of a man; and they four had the face of a lion on the right side; and they four had the face of an ox on the left side; they four had also the face of an eagle."*

Rev. 4: 6-7— *"And round about the throne, four living creatures full of eyes before and behind. And the first creature was like a lion, and the second creature like a calf, and the third creature had the face of a man, and the fourth creature was like a flying eagle."*

Ezekiel 1:19-19— *"As for their rims, they were high and dreadful and they four had their rims full of eyes round about. And when the living creatures went, the wheels went beside them; and when the living creatures were lifted up from the earth, the wheels were lifted up."*

Ezekiel 10: 12— *"And their whole body, and their backs, and their hands, and their wings, and the wheels, were full of eyes round about, even the wheels that they four had."*

It is obvious that the writers of the above passages were referring to the Zodiac as it appeared about 5000 years ago when the four bright stars associated with the bull, the eagle, the lion and the man were situated at the Vernal Equinox, the Autumnal Equinox, the Winter Solstice and the Summer Solstice and, according to Chinese legends, kept watch over all the others.

The Constellations of the Signs (in the order to be discussed later) are:

I   Virgo, the Virgin: the figure of a young woman, lying prostrate, with an ear of corn in one hand and a branch in the other.

II	Libra, the Scales: the figure of a pair of balances, with one end of the beam up and the other down, as in the act of weighing.
III	Scorpio, the Scorpion: the figure of a gigantic insect, noxious and deadly, with its tail and stinger uplifted in anger, as if striking.
IV	Sagittarius, the Bowman: the figure of a horse with the arms and head of a man—a centaur—with a drawn bow and arrow pointed at the Scorpion.
V	Capricornus, the Goat: the figure of a goat sinking down as in death, with the hind part of its body terminating in the vigorous tail of a fish.
VI	Aquarius, the Waterman: the figure of a man with a large urn, the contents of which he is in the act of pouring out in great stream from the sky.
VII	Pisces, the Fishes: the figures of two large fishes in the act of swimming, one to the northward, the other with the ecliptic.
VIII	Aries, the Ram (by some nations called the Lamb): the figure of a strong sheep,with powerful curved horns,lying down in easy composure, and looking out in conscious strength over the field around it.
IX	Taurus, the Bull: the figure of the shoulders, neck, head, horns, and front feet of a powerful bull, in the attitude of rushing and pushing forward with great energy.
X	Gemini, the Twins (or a man and woman sometimes called Adam and Eve): usually, two human figures closely united, sitting together in endeared affection. In some of older representations the figures of this constellation consist of two goats, or kids.
XI	Cancer, the Crab: the figure of a crab, in the act of taking and holding on with its strong pincer claws. In Egyptian astronomy, the scarabaeus beetle takes the place of the crab. It is represented as grasping and holding on to the ball in which its eggs are deposited.
XII	Leo, the Lion: the figure of a great rampant lion, leaping forth to rend. His feet are over the writhing body of Hydra, the Serpent, which is in the act of fleeing.

These major Constellations cover a large part of the visible heavens. They extend entirely around the earth, making and marking the Solar Zodiac. But these twelve great Constellations do not stand alone. Each has three minor constellations grouped around them, either on the north or south of the so-called "Zodiacal Belt".

The Minor Constellations are:

I Sign Virgo

1. Coma, the Infant, the Branch, the Desired One (erroneously Berenice's Hair)
2. Centaurus, a centaur, with dart piercing a victim.
3. Bootes, or Arcturus, the great Shepherd and Harvester, holding a rod and sickle, and walking forth before his flocks (erroneously called Bears).

II Sign Libra

1. Crux, or cross (called the Southern Cross) over which Centaurus is advancing.
2. Lupus, or Victim of Centaurus, slain, pierced to death.
3. Corona, the Crown (Borealis) which the Serpent aims to take, called the "Northern Crown."

III Sign Scorpio

1. Serpens, the Serpent, struggling with Ophiuchus.
2. Ophiuchus, the serpent holder, wrestling with the Serpent, stung in one heel by the Scorpion, and crushing it with the other.
3. Hercules, the Mighty Man, wounded in one heel, the other foot over the Dragon's head. In one hand he holds the Golden Apples and the three-headed Dog of Hell, in the other—the uplifted club.

IV Sign Sagittarius

1. Lyra, an Eagle, holding the Lyre, as in triumphant gladness.
2. Ara, the Altar, with consuming fire, burning downward.
3. Draco, the Dragon, the old Serpent, winding himself about the Pole in horrid kinks and contortions.

V Sign Capricornus

1. Sagitta, the Arrow (killing dart sent forth), the naked shaft of death.
2. Aquila, the Eagle, pierced and falling.

3.   Delphinus, the Dolphin, springing up, raised out of the sea.

VI Sign Aquarius

1. Picus Australis, the Southern Fish, drinking in the stream.
2. Pegasus, the winged horse, speeding, as with good tidings.
3. Cygnus, the Swan on the wing, going and returning, bearing the sign of the cross.

VII Sign Pisces

1. The Band, holding up the Fishes, but held by the Lamb, its doubled end fast to the neck of Cetus, the Sea-Monster.
2. Andromeda, a woman in chains, threatened by the serpents of Medusa's head.
3. Cepheus, a crowned king, holding a band and sceptre, with his foot planted on the pole-star as the great Victor and Lord.

VIII Sign Aries

1. Cassiopeia, the woman enthroned.
2. Cetus, the Sea-Monster, closely and strongly bound by the Lamb.
3. Perseus, an armed and mighty man with winged feet who is carried away, in triumph, the cut-off head of a monster full of writhing serpents.

IX Sign Taurus

1. Orion, a glorious Prince, with a sword girded on his side and his foot on the head of the Hare or Serpent.
2. Eridanus, the tortuous River, accounted as belonging to Orion.
3. Auriga, the Wagoner (rather the Shepherd), carrying a she-goat and two little goats on his left arm. He also holds cords, or bands, in his right hand.

X Sign Gemini

1. Lepus, the Hare (in some nations a serpent), the mad enemy under Orion's feet.
2. Canis Major, Sirius, the Great Dog, the Prince coming.
3. Canis Minor, Procyon, the Second Dog, following after Sirius and Orion.

XI Sign Cancer

1. Ursa Minor, anciently called the Lesser Sheepfold, close to and including the Pole Star.
2. Ursa Major, anciently called the Greater Sheepfold, in

connection with Arcturus, the guardian and keeper of the flock.

3. Argo, the Ship, the company of travellers under the bright Canopus, their Prince. These are the brave Argonauts, returning with the Golden Fleece.

XII Sign Leo

1. Hydra, the fleeing Serpent, trodden under foot by the Crab and Lion.
2. Crater, the Cup or Bowl of Wrath, upon the Serpent.
3. Corvus, the Raven or Crow, the bird of doom, tearing the Serpent.

This makes twelve major and thirty-six minor constellations— forty-eight in all. These forty-eight figures, in various forms, have been perpetuated in all astronomical records of the earliest civilizations. This suggests a common source, existing even before their time. Additional figures have since been added by modern philosophers; figures which are meaningless in this study. Among these additions are: the Sextant, the Giraffe, the Fox and Goose, the Fly, the Greyhounds, the Horned Horse, the Lynx, the Bird of Paradise, Noah's Dove, the Sculptor's Workshop, the Clock, the Painter's Easel, and such like, having no connection whatever with the primitive constellations.

THE MODERN LIST OF CONSTELLATIONS
[as standardized by the International Astronomical Union in 1928]

Name in Latin	Name in English	Name in Latin	Name in English
Andromeda	Princess	Lacerta	Lizard
Antlia	Air Pump	Leo	Lion
Apus	Bird of Paradise	Leo Minor	Little lion
Aquarius	Water Bearer	Lepus	Hare
Aquila	Eagle	Libra	Balance (scales)
Ara	Altar	Lupus	Wolf
Aries	Ram	Lynx	Lynx (bobcat)
Auriga	Charioteer	Lyra	Lyre (harp)
Bootes	Herdsman	Mensa	Table mountain
Coelum	Graving tool	Microscopium	Microscope
Camelopardalis	Giraffe	Monoceros	Unicorn
Cancer	Crab	Musca	Fly
Canes Venatici	Hunting dogs	Norma	Carpenter's level
Canis Major	Big dog	Octans	Octant
Canis Minor	Little dog	Ophiuchus	Holder of serpent
Capricornus	Sea goat	Orion	Hunter
Carina	Keel of ship	Pavo	Peacock
Cassiopeia	Queen	Pegasus	Winged horse
Centaurus	Centaur	Perseus	Perseus (hero)
Cepheus	King	Phoenix	Legendary bird
Cetus	Whale	Pictor	Easel
Chamaeleon	Chameleon	Pisces	Fishes
Circinus	Compass	Piscis Austrinus	Southern fish
Columba	Dove	Puppis	Stern of ship
Coma Berenices	Bernice's hair	Pyxis	Compass of ship
Corona Australis	Southern crown	Reticulum	Net
Corona Borealis	Northern crown	Sagitta	Arrow
Corvus	Crow	Sagittarius	Archer
Crater	Cup	Scorpius	Scorpion
Crux	Southern cross	Sculptor	Sculptor's tools
Cygnus	Swan, N cross	Scutum	Shield
Delphinus	Dolphin	Serpens	Serpent
Dorado	Swordfish	Sextans	Sextant
Draco	Dragon	Taurus	Bull
Equuleus	Little Horse	Telescopium	Telescope
Eridanus	Po River	Triangulum	Triangle
Fornax	Furnace	Triangulum Aus.	Southern triangle
Gemini	Twins	Tucana	Toucan
Grus	Crane	Ursa Major	Big Bear
Hercules	Hercules	Ursa Minor	Little bear
Horologium	Clock	Vela	Sail of ship
Hydra	Sea serpent	Virgo	Virgin
Hydrus	Water snake	Volans	Flying fish
Indus	Indian	Vulpecula	Fox

CONSTELLATIONS of SPRING

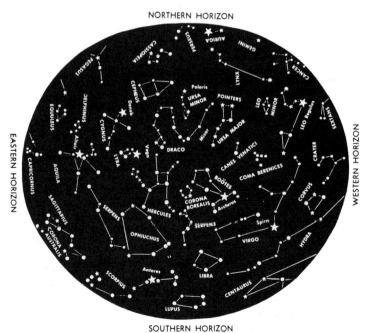

CONSTELLATIONS of SUMMER

NORTHERN HORIZON

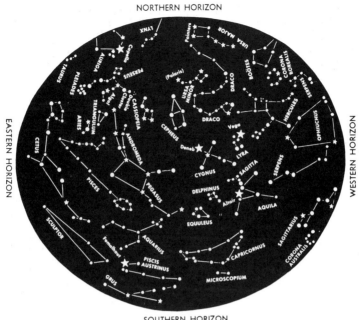

EASTERN HORIZON

WESTERN HORIZON

SOUTHERN HORIZON

CONSTELLATIONS of AUTUMN

NORTHERN HORIZON

EASTERN HORIZON

WESTERN HORIZON

SOUTHERN HORIZON

CONSTELLATIONS of WINTER

"Lift up your eyes on high, and behold who hath created these things: ...for that he is strong in power; not one faileth."

THE DIVINE ORIGIN OF THE ZODIAC

"And God said; Let there be lights in the firmament of the heaven to divide the day from the night; and let them be for signs, and for seasons, and for days, and years:"

Genesis 1:14

When God created the heavenly worlds He said, *"and let them be for signs".* A sign is something arbitrarily selected and appointed to represent some other thing. To make any sense of the creative record, we must admit that God intended these orbs of light as expressions of some special teaching; something different from what is naturally deducible from them.

In the Book of Job (generally believed to be the oldest book in the Bible) the names of several stars and constellations are mentioned as being both ancient and well known. We do not know, precisely, who Job was. He is referred to by Ezekiel in the Old Testament (bracketed with Noah and Daniel) and by James in the New Testament; *"Ye have heard of the patience of Job"* (James 5:11). In all 42 chapters of the Book of Job there is not one reference to Israelitish history, nor to the Law. This suggests that the writer lived in an earlier time. He lived before the destruction of Sodom and Gomorrah, hence, before Abraham.

From repeated astronomical allusions contained in the Book of Job, various mathematicians have calculated that Job lived and wrote somewhere about 2150 B.C. This date would carry us back more than 1000 years before Homer and about 1500 years before Thales, the first of the Greek philosophers. And yet, in the time of Job, the heavens were already charted and arranged astronomically in the manner described in the preceeding chapter. The Zodiac existed, with constellations and stars contained therein named; the figures drawn and recorded. Early Hebrews were conversant with these star charts and were impressed with their significance.

In the Book of Job, God challenged Job: *"Canst thou bring forth Mazzaroth [the constellations of the Zodiac] in his season?"* (Job 38:32)
Obviously man could exercise no control over the movements of the constellations, but must await each sign in the order of its season.

The constellation Draco (or Dragon) is identified by a passage in Job, *"By his spirit he hath garnished [made bright or beautiful]*

27

the heavens; his hand hath formed the crooked [or fleeing] serpent" (Job 26:13). Job also speaks of Arcturus and Orion (Job 9:9); the Pleiades (Job 38:31) and Cetus, the sea-monster (Leviathan) (Job 41:1). The manner of writing suggests that even in Job's day educated men were familiar with these heavenly signs.

Job describes the power, majesty, and works of God. He informs us that God is responsible for the naming and placing of these constellations. The Psalmist also states that God named the stars, *"He telleth the number of the stars; he calleth them all by their names"* (Psalms 147:4). A similar statement is made by the prophet Isaiah who declares: *"Lift up your eyes on high, and behold who hath created these [stars], that bringeth out their host by number: he calleth them all by names by the greatness of his might, for that he is strong in power; not one faileth"* (Isaiah 40:26).

In the fifteenth chapter (v. 5) of Genesis, the stars are spoken of as having been numbered (named) before Abraham's time. Stars are used (symbolically) to illustrate God's promise to Abraham that his decendants would be an innumerable number: *"And he brought him forth abroad, and said, Look now toward heaven, and tell the stars, if thou be able to number them: and he said unto him, So shall thy seed be".* This is not to be confused with the singular *"Seed"* (Christ) in whom *"shall all the nations of the earth be blessed* (Genesis 26:4).

The ancient Persian and Arabic traditions ascribe the invention of astronomy to Adam, Seth and Enoch. According to the Scriptures, Adam was the first in perfect fellowship with the Divine Intelligence. He knew all things that came before him by an intuitive divine insight into their true nature. He needed no instructors, for his whole being was in thorough accord with God; he was the complete image of God. His wisdom and understanding were undoubtedly higher, by far, than that of any man of the earlier creations. He excelled any of his own posterity.

It is also a matter of inspired record that God gave Adam special revelations. After the fall, God made known to Adam His purposes concerning the Serpent and the Seed of the woman. The revelation contained the whole Gospel including the promises. This knowledge was not given to Adam solely for himself or his posterity. He was to make it known to all the races of creation.

This agrees with writings of the most honored of the ancient philosophers and historians; those who delved the deepest into the origins of humanity. Baleus wrote concerning Adam and his fellowship with God: "He was the first that discovered the motions of the celestial bodies and all other creatures. From his school proceeded whatever good arts and wisdom which were afterward propagated by our father unto mankind; so that whatever astronomy, geometry and other arts contain in them, he knew the whole thereof." Moreri relates the tradition that "Adam had a perfect knowledge of sciences, and chiefly of what related to the stars, which he taught his children."

Adam and his immediate descendants lived hundreds of years. So they had ample time for observations and study; time to devise a means of recording and transmitting to all men the Creator's plan for humanity. The canopy of virgin stars was over them, just waiting to be named, grouped, and defined with certain symbols of the ideas they wished to convey. In this way, they could transmit and explain to their posterity the names and figures assigned to each star-grouping. Among the objects of Nature, none could have been selected as appropriately as the stars, for the purpose of recording and conveying unchanging ideas to distant ages. Their message was utterly imperishable as long as man was cognizant of the Divine nature of the Zodiac.

According to the historian Josephus and more ancient recorders, Adam and his son, Seth, are credited with the invention of letters. They were also the inventors of that peculiar wisdom which is concerned with the heavenly bodies, their appearance and arrangement. Enoch is also acclaimed as being the recorder of special wisdom relating to astronomy and prophecy. The Babylonians attributed the invention of astrology (astronomy) to Enoch. The Greeks knew Enoch as "Atlas". The Egyptians and Arabian writers made him the same as the elder Hermes (Hermes Trismegistus) the Triple Great Shepherd. Through him the wisdom of the stars and other sciences were handed down to his posterity.

Long standing traditions indicate that the ancient Biblical patriarchs were the first men to draw the celestial hieroglyphics. They named and grouped the stars, laid out the Zodiac and its constellations, and made the heavens a picture-gallery for all the world. Their legacy has enabled mankind to gaze and read the wondrous story of the promised Redeemer, the redemption and the redeemed.

The inspired prophets explained the star-signs as symbols of God's Divine revelation and promises. This would account for the sacred reverence in which all ancient people held the starry emblems. It would also explain the commonly held doctrines of antiquity; that the constellations were divine in origin and sacred in character. Even as the early nations lapsed into idolatry, worshipping the stars and ascribing to them all sorts of divine and prophetic virtues, they still believed the mysterious symbols were manifestations of one supreme and eternal deity.

Some of the earliest records dealing with the stars are the Chaldean Genesis tablets, recovered from the ruins of ancient Assyrian and Babylon. They date over 2000 years before the Christian era and are almost the same in substance as the Mosaic account of creation. The fifth tablet of the series relates how God created the constellations of the stars, the signs of the Zodiac (known by the heathen as Mansions - the stations or resting places of the 7 planets) the planets, the moon and the sun. This parallels the Bibical account that God placed the starry lights in the firmament and said: *"Let them be the signs"* (Genesis 1:14). The Book of Job tells us: *"by His Spirit He hath garnished the heavens* (Job 26:13).

Without question, the names by which the constellations were known have come down from antiquity, The source of inspiration which resulted in the naming and meaning of the pictorial groupings is implied as coming from God Himself. Historical astronomy claims mythology fathered these remarkable delineations of the heavenly bodies. But - it is evident that classic fables and myths, surrounding the constellations, are mere corruptions and imitations of an older and original composition.

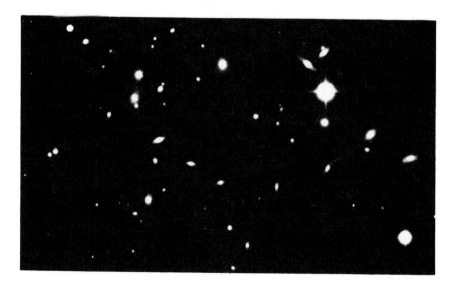

THE SIGNS OF THE ZODIAC

The twelve "Signs" of the Zodiac constitute twelve graphic chapters in a picturesque "book" of Divine Revelation. This message that God, by His Spirit, caused to be written in the sky is as one (by the same Spirit) with what He has caused to be written in His Word. If this premise is true then we should find a correlation between the star-figures and the Scriptures. There are remarkable similarities between the imagery and symbolism of the astronomical system of the constellations and the message recorded in the Holy Scriptures.

In examining the constellations, we are somewhat hindered by having to use the modern Latin names which they bear today. This is also the case with some of the Biblical names, translated from the Septuagint and the Vulgate. These were not always the Divine names, according to the Hebrew Canon. Then too, there are a few instances in which the original pictures seems to have been lost. However, the meaning of the ancient star-names makes it possible to restore the original figure and its symbolism.

Because the Zodiac is a circle and a circle has no beginning nor ending, the natural question is: Where should we break this circle and begin our story? A clue to the solution is found in the ceiling of the Portico of the Temple of Esneh in Egypt. An ancient circular Zodiac, there, shows a sphinx, having the head of a woman and the body of a lion, placed between the constellations of Virgo and Leo. This figure unites the beginning and the ending of the Zodiac (Modern astronomy starts with Aries the Ram). Since the word "Sphinx" means "to bind closely together" it was evidently designed to show where the two ends of the Zodiac were to be joined together, where the great circle of the heavens begins and ends.

Beginning with the woman - Virgo, the Virgin - and ending with Leo, the Lion, the twelve Signs (Constellations) of the Zodiac portray a pictorial story paralleling the Bible. The story is of the Redeemer, born as the Seed of a virgin. After being wounded, He returns as the Coming One, to crush the Serpent's head and to judge and rule in righteousness. Each of the minor constellations portrays the many details of this celestial message. This will be made clearer as we proceed to explain the story in the stars. We will compare it with the same truth which was afterwards written down in the Scriptures. So - let us proceed to a study of the constellations, remembering that the pictures are arbitrary. Nothing in the star-groupings themselves even suggests the figures.

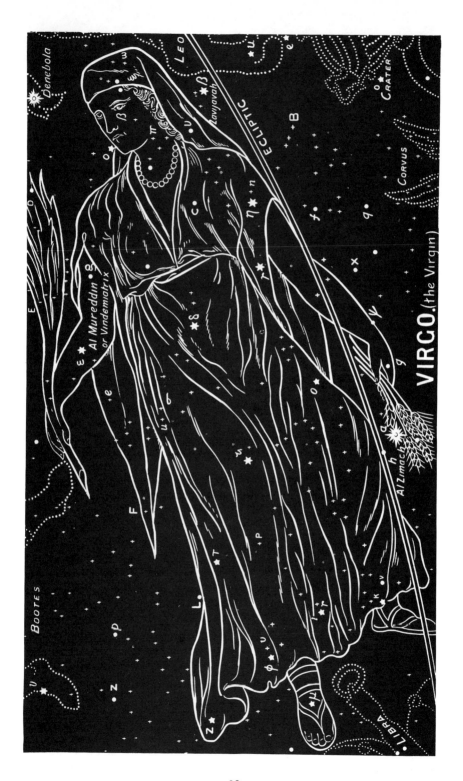

VIRGO.(the Virgin)

CHAPTER I - CONSTELLATION VIRGO [the Virgin]

Consists of 110 stars: one of the 1st magnitude: six of the 3rd: ten of the 4th, etc.

Virgo is pictured as a woman with a branch in her right hand and some ears of corn in her left hand. The name of this sign in Hebrew is "Bethulah", which means "a virgin": in Greek, "Parthenos","the maid of virgin pureness": in Arabic, "Adarah", "the pure virgin". All the traditions, names and mythologies, connected with this sign, recognize and emphasize the virginity of the woman. But, the greater wonder is that motherhood attends the virginity. About one hundred years before Christ, an altar was found in Gaul with this inscription: "To the virgin who is to bring forth". This woman in the sign is the holder and bringer of an illustrious Seed.

In the Zodiac of Denderah, in Egypt, Virgo is also represented with a branch in her hand. To the Egyptians the woman was represented as Isis, the wife of Osirus and was called "Aspolia", which means "ears of corn" or "the seed". The Greeks, likewise ignorant of the Divine origin and teaching of this sign, represented Virgo as "Ceres" with ears of corn in her hand.

The corn and the branch denote a two-fold nature of the Coming Seed. The first coming as the incarnate fulfillment of Isaiah 7:14, as quoted in Matt. 1:23, *"Behold a virgin shall be with child, and shall bring forth a son, and they shall call his name Emmanuel, which being interpreted is, God with us"*.

The bright star in the ear of corn in her left hand is called in Arabic, "Al Zimach", meaning "the branch". Zechariah writes of this branch: *"For behold, I will bring forth my servant the Branch"* (Zech. 3:8), described in the words of God, *"Behold my servant"* (Isaiah 42:1). It is significant that Christ referred to Himself as the corn, or seed of wheat, which needed to fall and die in order to attain its proper fruitfulness (John 12:23-24).

One of the stars in the branch is called "Al Mureddin" which means, "Who shall come down" or "who shall have dominion".

Psalms 72:8 states: *"He shall have dominion also from sea to sea"*. This star is also known by the Chaldee word, "Vindermiatrix" which means " the son " or "branch who cometh". An emblem of Christ, much employed by the prophets, was the branch, root, bough or sprout of a plant. Thus we find Christ described as the Rod from the stem of Jesse and a Branch out of his roots (Isaiah 11:1). He is the Branch of Righteousness, the Branch of the Lord, God's servant the Branch (Jer. 23:5; Isaiah 4:2; Zech. 3:8; 6:12).

The language of the prophecies is thus identical with the symbols in this sign. The doctrine of the Christian religion is that without Christ, and the redemption wrought by Him, all humanity is fallen and helpless in sin. There is none other name under heaven given among men, whereby we must be saved (Acts 4:12). Even Mary, herself, needed the mediatorial achievements of her glorious Seed to gain access to God, the Father. This too is symbolized in the Sign of Virgo, as the woman lies prostrate, helpless to stand upright. She holds forth the illustrious Branch, the Seed in whom is the only hope for a prostrate and fallen humanity.

The second coming (in glory and judgment) in the future, will be in fulfillment of Isaiah 9:6-7 (quoted in Luke 2:11 and 1:32-33),

"For unto us a child is born, unto us a son is given; and the government shall be upon his shoulder: and his name shall be called Wonderful, Counsellor, The mighty God, The everlasting Father, The Prince of Peace. Of the increase of his government an peace there shall be no end, upon the throne of David, and upon his kingdom, to order it, and to establish it with judgment and with justice from hence forth even for ever. The zeal of the Lord of hosts will perform this".

It should be pointed out that Virgo, in a broader prophetic sense, represented "the Virgin, the daughter of Zion"(Isaiah 37:22) which is another name for the nation of Israel (the whole 12 tribes). Throughout the Old and New Testament, Israel is often spoken of as the figures of a woman, the "wife" of Yahveh; the "virgin" of Zion (Jeremiah 14:17; 18:13; Amos 5:2, 2 John 1:1).

The significant points in this constellation are furthur expressed and defined in the three accompanying minor constellations. In Virgo, the name points to the woman as the prominent subject. Although the woman appears again, in the first of the three companion constellations, the name, "Coma", points to the child as the great subject.

34

1. COMA [the Infant]

Consists of 43 stars: 10 of the 4th magnitude: the remainder of the 5th, 6th, etc.

Ancient Zodiac's pictured this constellation as a woman with a child in her arms and called it "Comah", meaning "the desired" or "the longed for". Haggai 2:7 states *The desire of all nations shall come*.The ancient Egyptians called this sign, "Shes-nu", meaning "the desired son". They named the child "Horus". The Persian name of the woman denotes a pure virgin who is on a throne. She is nourishing an infant boy having the name "Ihesu" (Hebrew), significantly similar to the Greek name "Ieza", which is called "Christos".

In Luke we read, concerning the infant Christ, *"the child grew, and waxed strong in spirit, filled with wisdom, and the grace of God was upon him"* (Luke 2:40). Thus we find the child pictured as supported and nourished by what the Greeks represented as the virgin goddess of wisdom, righteousness and all the good arts.

COMA.(the Desired)

35

Modern star-maps have deviated from the original, in the case of this sign. Usually, they just have a woman's wig representing Coma. This representation is based on the Greek mythology. It pictures the hair of Berenice (the wife of the Egyptian king Euergetes) which was dedicated to the goddess Venus. Her hair, which was hung up in the Temple of Venus, was subsequently stolen. To comfort Berenice, Connon, an astronomer of Alexandria (B.C. 283-222), reported that Jupiter had taken it and made it into a constellation. The fact that the earlier Zodiac of Denderah (dating back to around 2000 B.C.) has no trace of any hair, but shows the figure of a woman and child, would indicate the later figures are a perversion. Shakespeare indicated an awareness of the true symbolism of the sign Coma. He spoke of the shooting of an arrow, up to heaven, "to the good boy in Virgo's lap" (Titus Andronicus, Act IV., Scene 3).

According to the Persian historian, Abulfaragius (1226-1286 A.D.), Zoroaster, of Zerdusht (the Persian) was a pupil of Daniel the Prophet. Zoroaster was given the prophecy that a new star would appear when He, whom Daniel foretold, should be born. In the writing "Zend Avesta", this new star was to appear in the sign of the Virgin. Tradition says it was the constellation Coma in which "the Star of Bethlehem" appeared. There may have been a Persian Magi among those who searched for the "Desire of all nations".

New stars, appearing suddenly, are not an unusual phenomenon. They have appeared again and again. The Greek astronomer Hipparchus recorded a new star so bright as to be seen in the daytime, in 125 B.C. Several early Christian writers, probably quoting from eye witnesses, wrote concerning a new star shining forth in the land of Jacob. Ignatius, Bishop of Antioch (A.D. 69) says: "At the appearance of the Lord a star shone forth brighter than all the other stars". Prudentius (4th cent. A.D.) describes the star as brighter than the morning star. As late as A.D. 1572 a new star appeared (in the constellation of Cassiopeia) that could be seen in the daylight. It faded from sight in 1574. One wonders if perhaps another star will shine forth from the constellation of Coma. This to be the "Sign" of the Son of Man in heaven (Matt. 24:30), when He shall be seen "*coming in the clouds of heaven with power and great glory*".

Thus, the constellation of Coma reveals that the coming "Seed" of the woman was to be a child born, a son given. But He was to be more than just a son. He was to have two natures in one person - God and man. This is shown in the next constellation.

2. CENTAURUS [the Centaur]

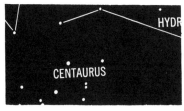

Consists of 35 stars: two of the 1st magnitude: one of the 2nd: six or the 3rd: nine of the 4th, etc.

The figure shown in this picture is that of a man's head, trunk and arms, coupled with a horse's body and legs. It faces eastward and is represented as charging with a levelled lance or spear in his hand. The spear is aimed at the heart of the victim (Lupus). The Greek name given to Centaurus was "Cheiron", which means "the pierced" or "who pierces". The figure of the Centaur indicates the two natures of the "Seed" of the woman.

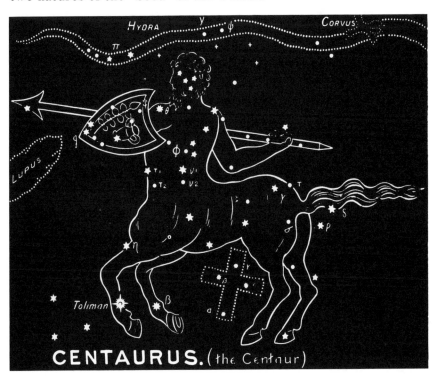

CENTAURUS. (the Centaur)

In both the Hebrew and the Arabic, the meaning of this constellation is "the despised". Isaiah wrote: *"He is despised and rejected of men; a man of sorrows, and acquainted with grief; and we hid as it were our faces from him; he was despised, and we esteemed him not"* (Isaiah 53:3). Another name for the constellation, in Hebrew, is "Asmeath", which means a "sin-offering" as in Isaiah 53:10: *"Yet it pleased the Lord to bruise him; he hath put him to grief: when thou shalt make his soul an offering for sin".*

Centaurus is one of the lowest of the constellations, being farthest south from the northern center. It is situated immediately over and surrounds the Southern Cross on three sides, and extends north of it to the coils of Hydra. The brightest star (in the horse's forefoot) is a binary, the smaller star being itself almost of the first magnitude. Taken together, the intrinsic brilliancy of the two stars is four times that of the sun. This star was known to the ancients as "Toliman", which means "the heretofore and hereafter", marking Him as the one "which is, and which was, and which is to come - the Almighty" (Rev. 1:8) Toliman has been observed to be growing rapidly brighter. It may be, therefore, one of the changeable stars, and its name may be taken as an indication of the fact it was known as such to the ancient astronomers. It was a prominent object of temple worship in Egypt.

A parallel between Christ and the centaurs of classic fables can be noted. Christ was wise, a good and powerful Healer, Instructor and Prophet, as were the centaurs. Centaurs were renowned as hunters and destroyers of wild bulls and wild boars, gifted in medicine, music and the arts of prophecy. Christ voluntarily took upon Himself the death of the Cross that others might live, as did the most noted of the mythical centaurs, Cheiron. He was fatally wounded by a poisoned arrow from heaven, not intended for him, while engaged in a good work. Though immortal in himself, he chose to die that another might live.

The story we are told by this figure is that the child, or "Promised Seed", should grow into manhood and as a man having two natures (Divine and Human) He should suffer and die. The following constellation further developes the marvellous story of the "Seed" of the woman.

3. BOOTES [the Coming One]

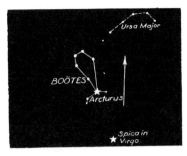

Consists of 54 stars: one of the 1st magnitude: six of the 3rd: eleven of the 4th, etc.

This constellation continues and defines the story of the constellation Virgo. The figure is of a strong man walking rapidly with a spear or rod in his right hand and a sickle in his left hand. The ancient Egyptians called him "Smat" which means "one who rules, subdues and governs". The Greeks, not fully recognizing the meaning of this sign, called it a ploughman and gave it the name "Bootes". The fallacy of this interpretation is apparent from the fact that the so-called plough, they depict, and the man are set in opposite directions. Neither does a man plough with an uplifted hand as pictured in the figure. However, the Greeks were not consistent to their idea of a ploughman for they also called this man "Arcturus", the watcher, guardian, or keeper of "Arktos" (the adjoining constellation). Modern zodiacs erroneously represent Arktos as the Great and Lesser Bears. Another and older corruption shows the man holding a leash which is attached to the two dogs, "Canes Venatici" (the Greyhounds) called "Asterion and Chara" (Hevelius 1611 - 1687). In all the ancient zodiacs we find Arktos representing "the flock, the sheepfold", thus showing that Bootes is not a ploughman, but the guardian and keeper of the sheepfold.

One of the most common and expressive symbols attached to Christ in the Scriptures is that of a shepherd. Isaiah prophesied of He who *"shall feed His flock like a shepherd"*. Peter also describes Him as the Shepherd and Bishop of our souls. Christ says of Himself: *"I am the good shepherd, and know my sheep, and am known of mine".* (John 10:11, 14); *"My sheep hear my voice, and I know them, and they follow me: And I give unto them eternal life; and they shall never perish, neither shall any man pluck them out of my hand"* (John 10:27-28).

The Hebrew meaning of the name of this constellation is "the coming". The sickle in his hand represents him as a reaper. John,

BOÖTES (the Coming One)

40

in his vision, beheld the final coming of the great Judge and Harvester to reap the harvest of the earth: *"And he that sat on the cloud thrust in his sickle on the earth and the earth was reaped"* (Rev. 14:16).

There is a wealth of meaning in the names of the stars making up this figure. Arcturus, a bright star in the figure's left knee, is mentioned in Job 9:9. It means "He cometh". The star "Al Katurop" (in the spear or rod) means "the branch, treading under foot". *"I will tread them in mine anger and trample them in my fury"* (Isaiah 63:3). Another star name means "who separates". In Matt. 25:32 Jesus declares He is the one who will separate: *"...and before him shall be gathered all nations and he shall separate them one from another, as a shepherd divideth his sheep from the goats"*. Other star-names mean, "who bruises", "the preserver" and "the pierced". *"They shall look upon me whom they have pierced"* (Zech. 12:10).

Bootes, together with the other constellations in the Sign Virgo, illustrates the coming of a Saviour, born of a virgin, "the desire of all nations", having two natures in one (God with us), slain for sin. Finally triumphant over death, He shall return again. Then He shall tread the winepress of the wrath of God and cleanse the earth of all evil and establish His rule of righteousness. This constellation completes the first "chapter" of the Celestial book. Like the Book of Genesis, it contains the outline of the whole volume as regards the Person of the "Coming One.". The continuing constellations, each amplifying the other, reveal the hope and trust of mankind that shines upon us, in our darkness, from God's everlasting stars.

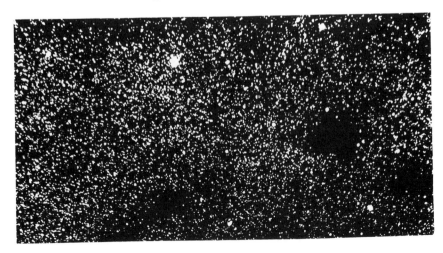

CHAPTER II—CONSTELLATION LIBRA [the Scales]

Consists of 51 stars: two of the 2nd magnitude: one of the 3rd: eight of the 4th, etc.

This constellation was blended by the Greeks with Scorpio, forming the out-stretched claws of that monster. It seems to have been separated from Scorpio, under the name of "Libra", in the time of Julius Caesar. However, the figure of the Scales or Balances, as an independent constellation, is found in all the Eastern and most ancient zodiacs. The down side is invariably slanted toward the deadly Scorpion.

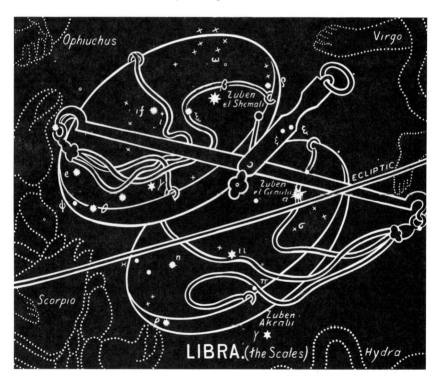

In Greek mythology, Libra represented the balances of Astraea, the Goddess of Justice, in which the fate of all mortal men must eventually be weighted. The Egyptians identified Libra with

42

the scale beam by means of which they measured the Nile flood. Sometimes they also associated it with the scales in which the human heart is to be weighed after death, the scales of justice. In India, Libra was also known as a balance, shown in their zodiac as a kneeling man holding up a pair of scales.

The scales convey the idea of purchase and the names of this sign indicate the range of meaning attached to it. In Hebrew it is called "Mozanaim", meaning "the Scales, weighing": In Arabic, "Al Zubena", meaning "purchase" or "redemption". In Coptic, "Lambadia", meaning "station of propitation" (from Lam-graciousness and badia-branch(. Its present name is the Latin "Libra", which means "weighing".

The four bright stars in this picture, by their names, supply us with the full meaning. The first star is "Zuben al Genubi, the price deficient". The second star is "Zuben al Shemali, the price which covers". The other two are "Al Gubi", meaning "heaped up high" and "Zuben Akrabi", meaning "the price of the conflict".

In the Persian Zodiac a man or woman lifts the scales in one hand, and grasps a lamb with the other. The lamb has the form of an ancient weight. All this clearly relates to defaults, defects and accusations involving penalties, prices and payments. These ideas are but a continuation of the story of the Seed of the woman, promised and appointed to recover fallen man from the Serpent's power. Recovery requires eternal justice; weighing the demerits and awards of sin on the one hand and the price paid for redemption on the other.

This thought is the basic theme of Christianity. Man, weighed in the balance, is found wanting. The price of redemption from sin is too high for mortal man to pay. One of the scales is up which says to universal man, *"Thou art weighed in the balances, and art found wanting"* (Dan. 5:27). But the other side of the scales is borne down, and with it the star named "the price that covers". What the accepted price was to consist of is more fully explained in the lesser constellations of Libra. These describe the great work of the Redemption, beginning with the Cross and ending with the Cross.

1. CRUX [the Cross]

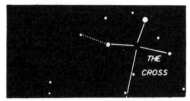

Consists of 5 stars: one of the 1st magnitude: two of the 2nd: one of the 3rd: one of the 4th, etc.

This figure consists of four bright stars placed in the form of a cross. It sits in the darkest section of the heavens, in the very lowest part of the sphere and is, by far, the most conspicuous star-group in the southern heavens. At the time of the birth of Jesus this Southern Cross, as it is called, was just visible in the latitude of Jerusalem. Since then, through the gradual recession of the Polar Star, it has become invisible at that latitude. Tradition says it disappeared from view at the time of Calvary.

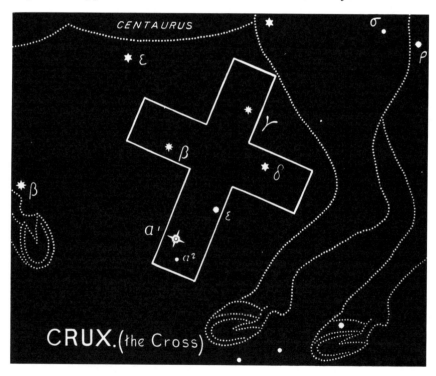

The Hebrew name of this constellation is "Adom", which means "cutting off". Daniel refers to the fact that *"After threescore and two weeks shall Messiah be cut off"* (Dan. 9:26). The Egyptians called this figure "Sera" which means "victory". To them it was a symbol of life-natural life given up and eternal life procured - perfect and complete. In the Zodiac of Denderah, Crux is represented as a lion with his head turned backward and his tongue hanging out of his mouth as if in thirst. Here we have but another symbol of Christ as the "Lion of the Tribe of Judah". One of the few expressions, made by Him as He died on the Cross, concerned His consuming thirst.

Ever since Jesus Christ bore the shame of the cross, it has been a sacred and most significant emblem to all Christian believers. To most Christians it is a symbol of life. To the Egyptians the scared "Tau" or cross was also a symbol of life and immortality. They had sacred cakes with the form of a cross upon them, which they ate in holy worship. It was but another form of the same idea - life and salvation through the Cross.

The Egyptians were not alone in their reverence of the cross. In the divine triad of Brahmanic deities, the second, the Son (the One who became incarnate in the man-god Kirshna) sits upon his throne cross-legged holding the cross in his right hand. He was worshipped as the god of deliverance from dangers and serpents. Also long before the Christian era, the sign of the cross was sacred to the Persians, Assyrians, Chinese, Mexicans, Peruvians, Scandinavians, Gauls and Celts. We cannot account for this ancient belief in the fabled virtues of the cross except as part of the original prophecies concerning a Saviour who was to suffer on it, conquer by it, and give eternal life through it.

The history of the pagan religions in all ages is replete with claims of divinity, from virgin-born gods to crucified saviours. In our day, scoffers of the Scriptures interpret this as evidence that Christianity has its origin in the paganism of the ancient religions. They name some dozen or more "crucified saviours" before Christ. However, it is more reasonable to believe that pagan religions usurped and perverted the ideas expressed in the stars to mask their teachings in an illusive veil of divinity, while Jesus Christ fulfilled the celestial prophecies.

So Crux stands among the starry symbols of ancient astronomy precisely as it stands in Christianity; a token of the price at which our redemption was to be bought. The next in the series of the heavenly signs gives us a fuller and clearer indication of that price.

2. Lupus [the Victim]

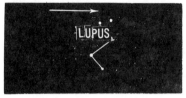

Consists of 22 stars: none greater than the 4th magnitude: most of the 5th and 6th magnitude.

Here we find the figure of an animal as slain by the spear of the centaur. It is in the act of falling down dead. Its Greek name is "Thera", "a beast" and "Lycos", a wolf. Its Latin name is "Victima" but more commonly called "the animal". The modern name of this sign is "Lupus" (a wolf) because in the modern zodiac it looks like a wolf, but there is no ancient authority for it. It may be any animal.

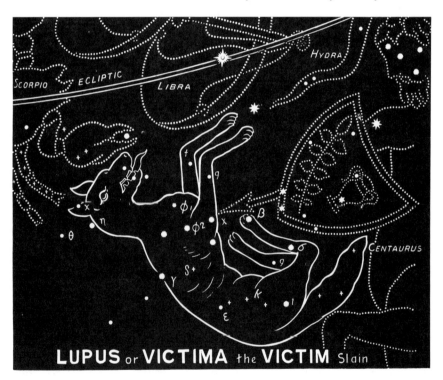

LUPUS or VICTIMA the VICTIM Slain

The ancient Egyptian Zodiac of Denderah perhaps best explains the meaning. There, the constellation is pictured as a little child with its fingers on its lips. Although Egyptian mythology refers to him as Horus, the beloved son of Osiris and the virgin, he was also called "Sura", meaning "A lamb". Isaiah prophesied of Jesus; *"He is brought as a lamb to the slaughter; and as a sheep before her shearers is dumb, so he opened not his mouth"* (Isaiah 53:7).

Men, in their ignorance, nailed Christ to the cross but it was He who gave Himself into their hands to do it. This is seen in the pictorial portrait of the victim slain by a spear, barbed in the form of the cross, coming from His own hand, symbolized by the Centaur. This is the important element in the mystical transaction on the Cross; that He sacrificed Himself. Jesus said: *"I lay down my life, that I might take it again. No man taketh it from me, but I lay it down of myself. I have power to lay it down, and I have power to take it again"* (John 10:17-18).

Therefore, we see in Lupus a celestial preview of the scriptual message - that He who knew no sin consented to become an offering for sin. He felt the agony and shame of the cross that we might have eternal redemption through His blood. *"And being found in fashion as a man, He humbled Himself, and became obedient unto death, even the death of the cross"* (Phil. 2:8). In substance, Lupus, or Victima, indicates the nature and payment of the price of redemption; *"The soul that sinneth, it shall die"* and *"without the shedding of blood is no remission"* (Ezek. 18:4, Heb. 9:22).

Christ's death by the Cross, marks the limit and farthest boundaries of the humiliation for human redemption. There is nothing lower than that in the history of man; and the first two minor constellations of the constellation of Libra (some ancient zodiacs combine them as one) are the southernmost constellations. But from the moment that Jesus gave up the ghost the price was paid, the whole debt was discharged, and everything gave token of change.

A man high in office and estate moved to take charge of His remains for an honorable burial. Imperial Rome lent its soldiers and its seal to guard and protect the place of their rest. The earth and sky gave signs of sympathy, and yielded attestations which drew even from heathen lips the confession of His divinity. The gates of Hell stood confounded before His majesty, and the doors of the grave gave way, and angels in white array stood round the spot to welcome His forthcoming in the powers of an endless life.

On the Cross, Jesus " was made a little lower than the angels for the suffering of death, crowned with glory and honor," (Heb. 2:9). But the shameful Cross was only the prelude to a glorious crown and throne which brings us to the third part of Libra.

3. CORONA BOREALIS [the Crown]

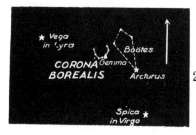

Consists of 21 stars: one of the 2nd magnitude: six of the 4th, etc.

Corona Borealis, or the "Northern Crown", is a semicircle of stars that rises just east of the northern part of Bootes. It is one of the constellations which can be easily recognized as bearing a resemblence to the object for which it is named. Most of the principal stars in this sign are of the white, twinkling kind, so that the crown is fully jewelled. The Arabic name of this sign is "Al Iclil", meaning: "an ornament" or "jewel".

CORONA.
(the Crown.)

The Hebrew name for this constellation is "Atarah", meaning a "royal crown". This star name is found quite a number of times in the Old Testament, but Isaiah 28:5 is one of the most fitting

48

references to the most perfect of all royal diadems: *"In that day, shall the LORD of hosts be for a crown [Atarah] of glory, and for a diadem of beauty, unto the residue of his people."* Here we see revealed that the "crown of glory" of the people of God is the Lord Himself. He, Himself, is the "diadem of beauty" of His elect.

Just as the Southern Cross follows and is connected with the Northern Crown, so the death of the great Redeemer is followed by his triumphant reward. Christ was brought up again out of death in immortal beauty and glory, *"and a crown was given unto him"* (Rev. 6:2). *"Thou are worthy...for thou wast slain and has redeemed us to God by thy blood..."* (Rev. 5:9). *"Wherefore God also hath highly exalted Him, and given Him a name which is above every name, that at the name of Jesus every knee should bow"* (Phil. 2:9-10).

Thus ends the concluding section of the second chapter, with glory to the Lamb. An extension of this prophecy is yet future when, at the Second Coming of the Redeemer, *"...every tongue should confess that Jesus Christ is Lord, to the glory of God the Father"* (Phil. 2:11).

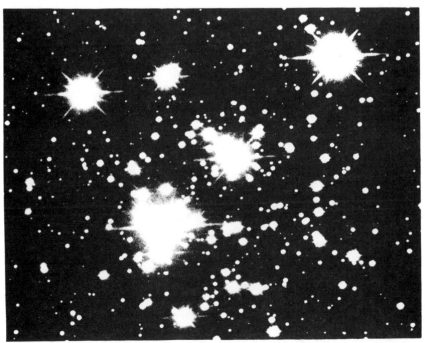

THE "JEWEL BOX" OF THE SOUTHERN MILKY WAY. A CLUSTER OF STARS NEAR THE SOUTHERN CROSS, FAINTLY VISIBLE TO THE UNAIDED EYE.

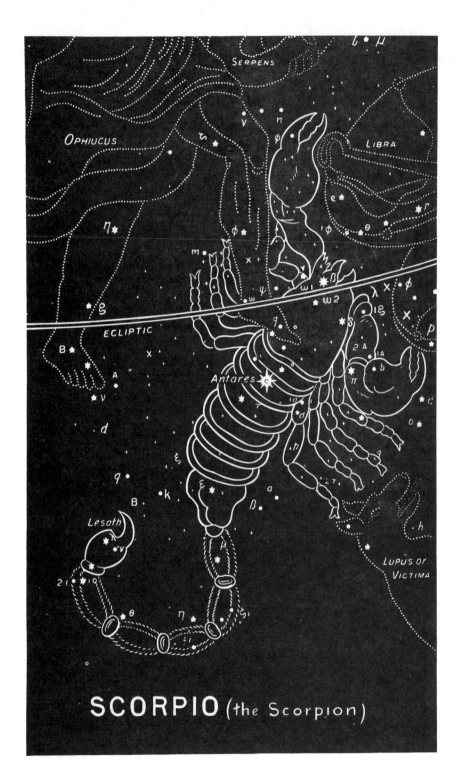

SCORPIO (the Scorpion)

CHAPTER III — CONSTELLATION SCORPIO   [Scorpion]

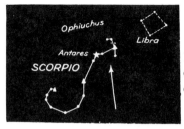

Consists of 44 stars: one of the 1st magnitude: one of the 2nd : eleven of the 3rd: eight of the 4th, etc.

In this constellation we have the figure of a mammoth scorpion, with its tail uplifted in anger. It appears to be trying to strike the man (Ophiuchus) who is struggling with a serpent. The man in turn is crushing the scorpion with his foot placed over the heart. The name of this constellation in Hebrew is "Akrab", and in Arabic; "Al Akrab"; both mean "the scorpion", also "wounding", "conflict" and "war". David uses the root of this word where he blesses God for teaching his hands to "war" (Akrab) (Psalms 144:1). In the Coptic, this sign is "Isidis", which means "the attack of the enemy" or "oppression". In the Zodiac of Denderah, Scorpio is represented by a monster serpent with a hundred heads, called "Typhon" or "Python".

Scorpio was everywhere an unfortunate, cursed and warlike constellation. The Mayas called it the "Sign of the Death-god". The Babylonians supposed Scorpio to have been among the monsters created by Tiamat when she rose in rebellion against the gods, and he was ever an opponent of the sun. To the Sumerians, Scorpio was known as "The Perverse One" or "The Lawless One".

The scorpion is a deadly enemy (as we learn in Rev. Chapter 9) with poison in its sting. The sting is called, in Hebrew, "Lesath" and in Chaldee "Lesha", both of which means "the perverse". The stars in the tail of the scorpion are also known as "Leshaa" or "Leshat". The brightest star (in the heart of the figure) and one of the reddest stars visible to the naked eye bears the ancient Arabic name of "Antares" which means, "the wounding" or "tearing". It was also known as the "Scorpion's Heart".

The figure, the names, and all the indications speak of a most malignant conflict, and of a deadly wounding in that conflict. Such a conflict is clearly set forth, in the Scriptures, between the serpent and the woman's Seed. Starting with the attempt to destroy all the males of the seed of Abraham (Exodus Chapt. 1), the efforts of Athaliah to destroy all the royal seed (II Kings 11:1)

Herod's slaying of all the male babes in Bethlehem the conflict develops into the real "wounding", received at the Cross, when the "Scorpion" struck the woman's Seed. This battle did not end at the Cross, but extends today to all Christians and involves the Kingdom of Jesus Christ.

To clearly indicate that this conflict only apparently ended in defeat (on the Cross), we have the first two minor constellations belonging to this sign presented as one picture. Actually the picture is threefold, for it includes the sign itself. Being thus joined, the scorpion, the serpent and the man, shows the ultimate triumphant of the serpent's opponent. Therefore, we must consider the first two sections of this third chapter together.

1. SERPENS [The Serpent]
2. OPHIUCHUS [the Serpent Holder]

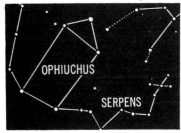

Consists (the two constelltions together) of 134 stars: two of the 2nd magnitude: fourteen of the 3rd: thirteen of the 4th, etc.

Here we have, showing the figure of a mighty man (Ophiuchus) wrestling with a gigantic serpent (Serpens) whose head is trying to reach a crown (Corona). The man is grasping the serpent with both hands, disabling the monster by his superior power and effectually holding him fast so that he cannot get the crown. With one foot lifted from the scorpion's tail as stung and hurt, he is in the act of crushing the scorpion's head with the other.

The man appears as the one who holds power over the serpent and over death, holding, disabling and destroying them though himself wounded in the conflict with them. Krishna, the Hindoo god (called an incarnation of Vishnu) is found represented in a similar fashion in two ancient sculptured figures. This would indicate that he may have originally symbolized the constellation Ophiuchus, but during the passage of the ages the true meaning of what was foretold became lost and the symbol itself became the fulfillment of the prophecy in the Hindoo religion.

What is really pictured here is the wrestling and agony which the Seed of the Virgin experienced in "the hour of the powers of darkness", as He himself explained, when He came to the final act of discharging the debt for the sins of a condemned world. It was the sting and poison of the great Scorpion (Satan), striking the Son of God, causing Him to suffer such great physical anguish that every pore issued blood.

The Greek name of the constellations of Ophiuchus, is itself from the Hebrew and Arabic name "Afeichus", which means, "the serpent held". The brightest star (in the man's head) is called, in Arabic, "Ras Alhegue" or "Ras al Hagus", meaning "the head of him who holds". The meaning of other star names in this constellation are "Triophas"; "treading under foot"; "Saiph" (in the man's foot); "bruised"; "Carnebus"; "the wounded"; "Megeros"; "contending".

In Greek mythology, Ophiuchus was known as "Aesculapius",

and was held to be one of the worthiest of the gods. He was described as "the Healer", "the Physician", "the Desired One", "the Health-giver", "The Beautifier with good health", "the One who brings cure" and "the Universal Remedy". (The symbol of the serpent entwined around him is to this day the symbol of the medical arts). All this is yet another perversion of the primitive truth that the Coming One, in overcoming the serpent should become the great healer of all mankind. Christ is the Resurrection and the Life; the great Healer; the heavenly Physician.

The serpent (Serpens) pictured held by the man (Ophiuchus) is, of course, to be construed with the Scorpion. The Hebrew name of the brightest star (in the Serpent's neck) is called Alyah, meaning "the accursed". Another name for the same star is "Unuk", meaning "encompassing". The next brightest star is Cheleb (Arabic), meaning "the serpent enfolding". This figure of a serpent has ever been the universal symbol and representative of that Evil Spirit which is called the "Dragon", that "Old Serpent", the "Devil", and "Satan". It is the symbol of the arch-enemy of all good, the opponent of God and the Deceiver of men. The Scriptures, everywhere, assure us of the existence of a personal Devil and Destroyer, just as it everywhere described a personal God and Redeemer. The doctrine of a Saviour necessarily implies the doctrine of a Destroyer. Men may doubt and question, and treat the idea of a personal Devil as a foolish myth. People may jest of it, but the doctrine is found in the oldest, worthiest, and most divine record ever made for human enlightenment; a doctrine held in the common belief of all nations and peoples, from the beginning of mankind. Here we have it pictured and repeated at every turn of the starry configurations, precisely as we find it presented in the sacred Scriptures. We should honestly receive and believe it for some day we will find this story of the Serpent to be a terrible reality. We do not necessarily see the physical image of the Devil and Satan; often he is only the dark and subtle intelligence operating within a person to deceive and destroy. No sooner did Christ come into the world than the Dragon sought to devour Him through Herod.

Satan symbolized in the constellation of Serpens by the serpent, is pictured looking up and reaching forth to seize the crown (Corona Borealis). He is being kept from taking it only because he is held fast by Ophiuchus, representing Jesus Christ. A further confirmation that we are correctly interpretating this figure can be seen in the fact that in the preceeding picture (chapter II) a celestial crown was held forth for Him who was to suffer on the cross.

3. HERCULES [the Mighty Man].

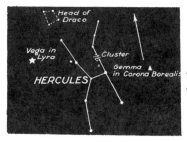

Consists of 113 stars: seven of the 3rd magnitude: seventeen of the 4th: etc.

The figure in this constellation is of a mighty man, down on one knee, with his heel uplifted as if wounded. He wears the skin of a lion he has slain and is holding a great club in his right hand. In his left hand is a three-headed creature (Cerberus - placed by Hevelius 1611-1687) and his left foot is set directly on the head of the great Dragon.

In the Zodiac of Denderah we also find a human figure with a club, for this sign, named "Bau", which means "who cometh". On most atlases the man is called by the Roman name "Hercules" although the Greeks called him "Herakles". They worshipped and honored him as the greatest of all their hero-gods. In Arabic, the man is called "Al Giscale", meaning "the strong one". The Phoenicians reverenced this man nearly two hundred years before the time of the Greeks and honored him as representing a "saviour". Sayce (the British Orientalist) traces the legend of him in Chaldee four thousand years ago.

The brightest star (in his head) is named Ras al Gethi, meaning "the Head of him who bruises". The next (in the right arm pit)is Kornephorus, meaning"the Branch, kneeling". Another star (in the right elbow) is called "Morsic"; "the wounding". The names and meanings of two other stars are "Maasyn" (in the upper part of the left arm), "the sin-offering", and "Caiam", or "Guiam" (in the lower part of the right arm), "punishing" and in Arabic "treading under foot".

According to the mythic accounts, Hercules was the god-begotten man who, from cradle to death, accomplished the most difficult and wonderful feats in the line of vanquishing great evil powers. He overcame the lion begotten from Typon, the many-headed Hydra sprung from the same parentage, the brazen-footed and golden-horned stag, the Erymanthean boar, the vast filth of the Augean stables, the swarms of life-destroying

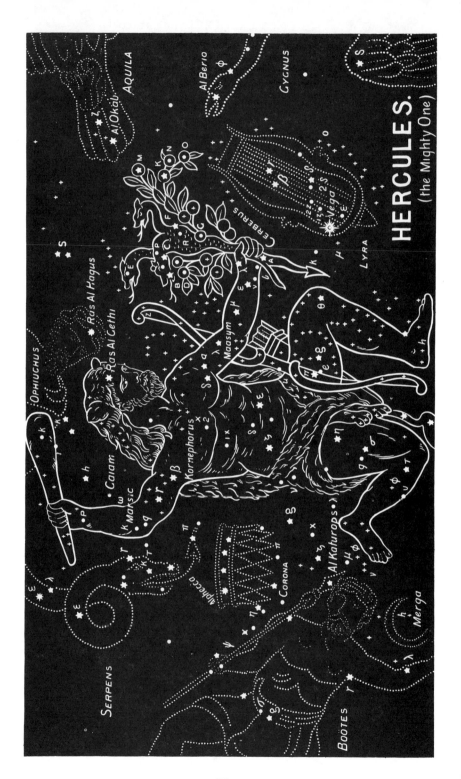

HERCULES.
(the Mighty One)

Symphalian birds, the man bull of Crete which no mortal dared look upon, the flesh-eating mares of Diomedes, the queen of the devastating Amazons, the triple bodied Geryones and his dog, the Dragon which guarded the apples of the Hesperides and the three-headed snaky monster which kept the gates of hell.

A prevailing theory, held by many, is that the story of Hercules is a purely Greek invention, but it has been found to date back, in all its aspects, to Egypt, Phoenica and India; to a time long anterior to the Greeks. By their own admission, the Greeks realized (as regards Greek mythology) that much had been "added after the mythical style" (Aristole in his Metaphics) to replace what had been lost of ancient wisdom. Other philosophers have noted that mythology contains only the fragments of traditions, which transmitted the knowledge of divine things possessed in the earliest times.

In spite of the ancient perversions which have woven fables and gods around the ancient names, their meanings, we can still see, foretold the mighty works which the Seed of the woman, (Jesus Christ) should perform, *"Thou shall tread upon the lion and adder, the young lion and the dragon shalt thou trample under foot"* (Psalms 91:13).

It is not difficult to see how the original star-picture must have been a prophetic representation of Him who shall destroy the Old Serpent and open the way again, not to fabled "apples of gold", but to the "tree of life itself". It was He who, though suffering in the mighty conflict, being brought to His knees even going down into the "dust of death"; was resurrected to life. It was He who in coming glory will wield His victorious club, subdue all His enemies and make this groaning and afflicted world the dwelling place of God in His coming Kingdom. The Psalmist describes the Coming King *"And thy majesty ride prosperously, because of truth and meekness and righteousness; and thy right hand shall teach thee terrible things. Thine arrows are sharp in the heart of the King's enemies; whereby the people fall under thee. Thy throne, O God, is for ever and ever: sceptre of thy kingdom is a right sceptre"* (Psalms 45: 4-6). What is pictured in these glowing words is what we find in our next constellation of the Zodiac.

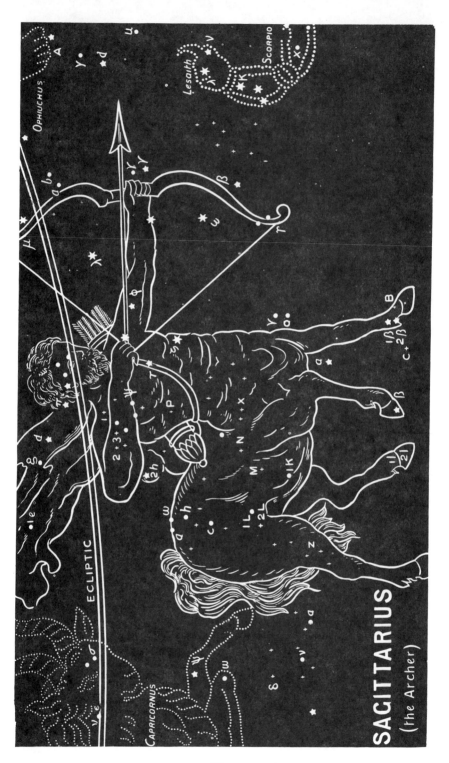

SAGITTARIUS
(the Archer)

CHAPTER IV – CONSTELLATION SAGITTARIUS

[the Archer]

Consists of 69 stars: five of the 3rd magnitude (all in the bow): nine of the 4th, etc.

In the Sign Sagittarius, we again have the figure of a Centaur indicating the double-natured Seed of the Virgin-the Son of God as the Son of Man. The figure is that of a mighty warrior with a bow and arrow, riding forth majestically. The barbed arrow in his bow is aimed at the heart of the Scorpion. John the Revelator, in his apocalyptic vision, sees the same mighty Conqueror going forth:

"And I saw, and behold a white horse; and he that sat on him had a bow, and a crown was given unto him, and he went forth conquering, and to conquer" (Rev. 6:2).

The Psalmist also wrote of this Archer who shall presently come forth, all powerful, to war with the whole Serpent brood, *"But God shall shoot at them with an arrow; suddenly shall they be wounded. So they shall make their own tongue to fall upon themselves: all that see them shall flee away. And all men shall fear, and shall declare the work of God, for they shall wisely consider of his doing"* (Psalm 64:7-9).

In Hebrew, the name of this constellation is "Kesith", which means "the Archer"; in Arabic, "Al Kaus", meaning "the arrow". In Hebrew, the names of the two brightest stars are, significantly, "Naim", which means "the gracious one", and "Nehushla", meaning "the going" or "sending forth". In ancient Akkadian the name of this picture is "Nun-Ki", meaning "Prince of the earth". Under this constellation in the ancient Zodiac of Denderah is the word "Knem" (in hieroglyphics) which means "He conquers".

According to Greek myths, "Cheiron", as the Greeks called this sign, was the great teacher of mankind in heavenly wisdom, medicine and all noble arts. He was a gracious King, especially blessed of God, whose name every generation shall remember and whom the people shall praise for ever and ever. Although the Greeks recognized the attributes expressed by this sign and its star-names, the original story had been lost by their time.

The Hindoos, although lacking understanding of the promised Seed of the woman, did recognize the nature of the meaning of this constellation. In the Indian sacred books there is a "tenth avatar" predicted, when Vishnu, the second in the divine Triad, is to come as a man on a white horse, overthrowing his enemies and rooting out all evil from the earth. The same story is told in Revelation (in the New testament) when the "King of Kings" and "Lord of lords" comes forth to do battle against the Beast, the false Prophet and all their armies in that great "Day of the Lord". He comes in the form of a man sitting upon a white horse, in righteousness, judging and making war, the same as in Sagittarius.

We must understand the Archer is at war with the Scorpion and all the evil creatures associated with it, and his going forth is for their destruction. The figure is representative of the office and purpose of the glorified Christ-to pierce and wound the Serpent, to destroy all his works and power, and to disable him forever. The first of the three minor constellations in the sign Sagittarius takes up the subject of praise for the Conqueror.

M20, THE TRIFID NEBULA IN SAGITTARIUS.

1. LYRA [the Harp]

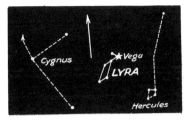

Consists of 43 stars: one of the 1st magnitude: one of the 3rd: five of the 4th: eight of the 5th: etc.

Modern atlases depict the figure in this sign by an eagle holding the harp, or a harp placed over an eagle; representing triumphant song springing from the eagle (the vanquisher and destroyer of the serpent). In the older zodiacs the constellation is marked by the figure of an eagle or hawk (the enemy of the serpent) who darts forth upon his prey from the heavenly heights with great suddenness and power. The suddenness again accords with the sayings ascribed to Christ in the Gospel: *"Behold, I come quickly and my reward is with me"* (Rev. 22:12) and *"For when they shall say, Peace and safety; then sudden destruction cometh upon them"* (I Thess. 5:3).

LYRA. (the Harp)

Lyra contains one of the most superb of all the first magnitude stars. Its name is "Vega", which means "He shall be exulted". Its actual magnitude is very great, probably a hundred times that of our sun. About fourteen thousand years ago Vega was the north Polar Star, and, in consequence of the precession of the equinoxes, it will occupy the same position about eleven thousand years hence.

Two other conspicuous stars, between the 4th and 5th magnitudes, are Shelyuk, which means "an eagle" and Sulaphat, meaning "springing up" or "ascending" - as in praise.

The placing of the harp, the oldest of stringed instruments (known during the time of Adam - Gen 4:21) following Sagittarius connects pre-eminent gladness, joy, delight and praise with the actions of this great Archer, with his bow and arrow. Thus he appears in this sign - answering to the Lamb as John held Him in the fourth and fifth chapters of Revelation, receiving the universal song of praise: *"Blessing, and honour, and glory, and power, be unto Him that sitteth upon the throne and unto the Lamb for ever and ever"* (Rev. 5: 13).

ARA. (the altar.)

2. ARA [the Altar]

Consists of 9 stars: three of the 3rd magnitude: four of the 4th, etc.

Nearly all the star-charts show the figure of an altar, covered with burning fire, to denote this constellation. The fire is burning downward, significantly, toward the lower regions of "darkness", called Tartarus, known as the "outer-darkness" (the area toward the covered and invisible south pole.) The word "ara" was sometimes used by the Greeks to imply a curse, or the effect of a curse (i.e. ruin, destruction).

In the Zodiac of Denderah, the figure is different but carries the same basic idea. There we have a throned human figure wielding a flail over a jackal, the unclean and cunning animal of darkness. The jackal, often identified with the dragon, is being threshed, bruised, punished and brought under dominion and judgment. The throned figure has a name (Bau) which signifies "the Coming One", the same as in Scorpio.

We can see depicted in this constellation a coming judgment, symbolizing the burning pyre and "the Coming One", enthroned with the threshing instrument. Revelation foretells of this overcoming of the Dragon, *"And he laid hold on the dragon, that old serpent, which is the Devil, and Satan, and bound him a thousand years"* (Rev. 20:2). The ultimate judgment then followed: *"And the devil that deceived them was cast into the lake of fire and brimstone, where the beast and the false prophet are, and shall be tormented day and night, forever and ever* (Rev. 20:10).

DRAGO. (the Dragon Cast down)

3. DRACO [the Dragon]

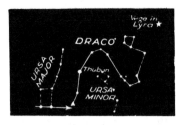

Consists of 80 stars: four of the 2nd magnitude: seven of the 3rd: ten of the 4th, etc.

The figure of this constellation is a great serpent wound about at least one-half of the northern sky. His tail alone extending over the territory of "the third part of the stars". The Greek name (Draco) for this sign means "trodden on"; *"The dragon shalt thou trample under feet"* (Psalms 91:13). In the Zodiac of Denderah, this sign is shown as a serpent under the forefoot of Sagattarius and is named "her-fent", which means "the serpent accursed".

The most prominent star (in one of the latter coils) is named in Hebrew, "Thuban", which means "the subtle". About 4600 years ago Thuban was the north Polar Star, and much closer to the true pole than Polaris is at the present time. This star is now below the 3rd magnitude, but it is believed to have once been as bright as Polaris. It still possesses great interest because the mysterious downward sloping passage in the Great Pyramid of Giza, in Egypt, points to the place that it occupied in the sky when it was the pole-star. It is believed that the star could then be seen by day as well as by night from the bottom of the passage deep beneath the foundation of that mighty pile of stone.

A bright star (in the head) is named "Ethanin" which means "the long serpent" or "dragon". Another bright star (also in the head) is called "Rastaban", meaning "the head of the subtle" (serpent). In the Arabic it is called "Al Waid", which means "who is to be destroyed". The Hebrew names of other stars and their meaning are: Grumian; "the subtle"; Giansar, "the punished enemy". The Arabic names of the stars in Draco have similar meanings; to name a few: "Al Dib," "the reptile"."El Athik," "the fraudful"; " El Asieh ", "the bowed down".

Draco thus represents the sly and creeping deceiver, the Devil, called the "Dragon", that old "Serpent". He destroys by stealth, smoothly gliding in to betray - insinuating his poison. The Dragon and the Serpent are one and the same, but are manifested in different ways. No man ever saw a dragon, living or dead, yet all men talk of the dragon. In all ages, this image or evil power has figured conspicuously in man's myths, traditions and in his art and literature; evil, symbolized by a dragon being vanquished by the works of ;ods, heroes and saints. Yet, there is nothing in earthly zoology to explain or account for such a creature.

Mythology says the Dragon is the power that guarded the golden apples in the famous Garden of the Hesperides, hindering men from getting them. Does not this symbolize the Devil, "the old Serpent, the Dragon" who deceived Adam and thus kept mortal men from the true fruits of the Tree of Life? Mythology says this Dragon was slain by Hercules. Isn't this portrayed in the astronomical sign of the promised Seed of the woman, the Coming One, who is pictured with His foot on the head of the Dragon?

Isaiah refers to the time when the Lord shall come - a ... *"great and strong sword shall punish leviathan the piercing serpent; and he shall slay the dragon..."* (Isaiah 27:1). The Psalmist also wrote of God breaking *"the heads of leviathan in pieces"* and breaking *"the heads of the dragons"* (Psalms 74:13-14).

Chapter IV ends the first section of the celestial book. We have seen pictured the Person, Work and Triumph of the illustrious Redeemer. The succeeding group, consisting of Capricornus, Aquarius, Pisces and Aries, with their accompanying minor constellations, relates to the fruits of His work; the prophecy of the promised deliverance.

CHAPTER V – CONSTELLATION CAPRICORNUS

[the Sea Goat]

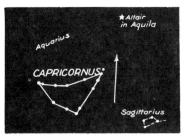

Consists of 51 stars: three of the 3rd magnitude: three of the 4th, etc.

In all the ancient zodiacs, this picture is shown as a fallen and dying goat with the tail of a fish - half goat and half fish. One leg of the goat is doubled under his body and the other is powerless to lift him up. The tail of the fish, on the other hand, seems to be full of vigor and life. Capricornus is the Latin name for this constellation and means not only "goat" but "atonement". Its Hebrew name is "Gedi", meaning "the kid" or "cut off".

The major star (in the horn) is named Al Gedi meaning "the kid" or "goat". Other stars have the same meaning. Deneb Al Gedi; "the sacrifice cometh"; Ma 'asad, "the slaying". Sa' ad al

CAPRICORNUS (the Goat)

Naschira, "the record of the cutting off".

In this constellation the thought, expressed, is the "atoning sacrifice". In the Scriptures, the goat is a sacrificial animal. Aaron "took the goat...and slew it, and offered it for sin"(Lev.9:15). And of the goat of the "sin-offering", Moses said: "...it is most holy, and God hath given it you to bear the iniquity of the congregation, to make atonement for them before the Lord"(Lev. 10:17). This was one of two goats. The other was not sacrificed, "and he shall let go the goat in the wilderness"(Lev. 16:22).

The dying goat is comparable with the falling and dying of Christ as the sin-offering referred to in the sign Hercules. Christ "was wounded for our transgressions, he was bruised for our iniquities"(Isaiah 53:5). "...he was cut off out of the land of the living: for the transgression of my people was he stricken"(Isaiah 53:8).

The living fish proceeding from the dying goat pictures a mystic procreation and a bringing forth. That which is brought forth is a fish, the familiar and well understood symbol of Jesus Christ. In the name and titles of the Seed of the woman - "Jesus Christ, the Son of God, our Saviour" - the initals in Greek form a name which signifies a fish.

The pagan myths concerning this constellation are many and varied. Pan and Bacchus are both connected to Capricornus, as well as Oannes, the half-fish god of the Babylonians and Dagon, the half-fish god of the Philistines. According to Philo, the name "Dagon" means "fruitfulness, the seed-producing". Dagon was to the Philistines, the same as Horus was to the Egyptians, having a human form in place of the goat. He was worshipped as the god of husbandry; the god of seeds and harvests. The Babylonians also referred to Capricornus as the "Father of Light" and sometimes identified him with their culture-god Ea who came to earth to benefit mankind.

In spite of such paganized and corrupted paraphrasing, the original primeval conception shines through; of Christ, Redeemer and Savior, fallen and dying in the Goat, but producing the living fish, the "great multitude, which no man could number"(Rev. 7:9) These are the redeemed that shall obtain eternal life through the death of their Redeemer.

The lesser constellations in this sign also reveal a prophetic knowledge which only He possessed, knowing that in the "fulness of the time...God sent forth His Son...to redeem them that were under the law"(Gal. 4:4-5).

1. SAGITTA [the Arrow]

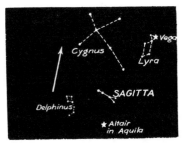

Consists of 18 stars: four of the 4th magnitude, etc.

Here is pictured an arrow, having left the bow being in flight. It is a heavenly arrow and He who shoots it is invisible. Its Hebrew name is "Sham," meaning "destroying"or"desolate". Taken alone, it projects little meaning, but placed in the context of the Goat and its associated signs, its interpretation can readily be seen. It is the death-arrow of Divine justice, which goes forth against all unrighteousness and sin. David speaks of the arrows of God: *"For thine arrows stick fast in me, and thy hand presseth me sore"* (Psalm 32:2).

There are many other stars in the heavens in a straighter line, which would better serve for an arrow, however, this constellation was known to the Arabians, Armenians, Persians, and the ancient Hebrews as the Arrow and this name has come down to us through the ages. The Latin equivalent, which is frequently used, is Sagitta. On a few of the early star-maps the Eagle was pictured with an arrow in his talons, which probably accounts for some of the modern pictures of an eagle holding one or more arrows in his claws.

Unlike the arrow of Sagittarius, which is reserved for the enemies of God, this arrow symbolizes the Word of God; the arrow of conviction for sin. The execution it does is shown in the fallen and dying goat, akin to the piercing and slaying of Christ Himself signifying the wounding and killing of sin in men's souls, it makes humble penitents of them, that they might live again in Christ. This idea is further expressed in the second minor constellation of Capricornus.

SAGITTA.(the arrow) AQUILA.(the Eagle) DELPHINUS.(the Dolphin)

2. AQUILA [the Eagle].

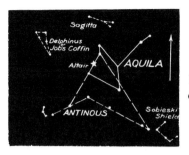

Consists of 74 stars: one of the 1st magnitude: five of the 3rd: one of the 4th, etc.

As in the case of the Arrow, we have another figure, whose message is difficult to understand, when taken alone: a pierced, wounded and falling eagle. Its principal star is Al Tair, which in Arabic means "the wounded". Its second star, Al Shain means "the scarlet-colored-covered with blood". The third, Tarared, means "the torn", while that of another, Al Okal, means "wounded in the heel".

There is no satisfactory explanation of the meaning of these star-names except to elaborate on the same ideas which we find symbolized in the sign of Capricornus. The Eagle is a royal bird and the natural enemy of the serpent. It is one of the Biblical symbols of Christ; *"Ye have seen what I did unto the Egyptians, and how I bare you on eagle's wings and brought you unto myself* (Ex. 19:4) *"As an eagle, stirreth up her nest, fluttereth over her young, spreadeth abroad her wings, taketh them, beareth them on her wings; so the Lord alone did lead him"* (Duet. 32:11, 12).

In this sign the noble Eagle, the promised Seed of the woman is shown pierced, torn and bleeding, that those in His image may be saved from death, protected and made to live forever. *"Thus it is written, and thus it behoved Christ to suffer, and to rise from the dead the third day, that repentance and remission of sins should be preached in His name"* (Luke 24:46, 47); *"...for thou wast slain, and hast redeemed us to God by thy blood out of every kindred, and tongue, and people, and nation"* (Rev. 5:9).

3. DELPHINUS [the Dolphin]

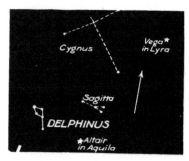

Consists of 18 stars; two of the 3rd magnitude: three of the 4th: one of the 5th, etc.

The figure of a vigorous fish leaping upward, in contrast to the eagle with its head downward, is the usual representation of this constellation. The Persians portrayed a fish and a stream of water, while the Egyptians had a vessel pouring out water. The Hebrew name of this constellation is "Dalaph", meaning "pouring out of water", but translates into Arabic as "coming quickly". Its Arabic name is "Scalooin", meaning "swift" (as the flow of water) and the sign was known to the Chaldeans as "Rotaneu", meaning "swiftly running".

In ancient mythology we find the dolphin was the most sacred and honored of fishes, no doubt because of the astral significance anciently ascribed to it. In some accounts, it was a dolphin which brought about the marriage of the unwilling Amphetrite with the god of the sea, and for this it received a place among the stars. The Bible reflects something of the original idea. Christ was the one, who, by His death and resurrection opened the way for Adam's race to be brought back into a fellowship with God.

The portrayal of the dolphin with its peculiar characteristics of rising up or leaping and springing out of the sea is allegorical of Jesus Christ, rising from the grave, *"the first fruits of them that slept"*(I Cor. 15:20). Having gone down into the waters of death on account of the sins of His people, He *"...was raised again for our justification "*(Rom. 4:25).

CHAPTER VI – CONSTELLATION AQUARIUS

[the Water Bearer]

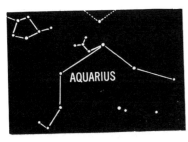

Consists of 108 stars: four of the 3rd magnitude, etc.

This is the figure of a man, holding a great urn in his left hand, from which is pouring out an inexhaustible stream of water. The water is flowing downwards into the mouth of a great fish, which receives it and swallows it all. Aquarius is the modern Latin name by which this sign is known. It has the meaning "the pourer forth of water".

The name of the principal star (in the right shoulder) is "Sa ad al Melik" meaning "record of the outpouring". A second star (in the other shoulder) is known as "Saad al Sund", "who goeth and returneth" or "the pourer out". A third star (in the lower part of the left leg) is called by the Hebrew name "Scheat" which means "who goeth and returneth". Another bright star (in the urn) has an Egyptian name "Mon" or "Meon" meaning "an urn".

Mythology calls the man "Ganymedes", the bright, glorified and happy One, so beautiful on earth that the great King and Father of gods carried him away to heaven on eagles wings to live in glory with immortals. Classic art associates him with an eagle and a bowl and, again, as the exalted companion of the eternal Father. Such descriptions obviously have their roots in Jesus Christ of whom the Father said; "Thou art my beloved Son, in whom I am well pleased" (Mark 1:11).

Following immediately after the constellations portraying atonement, Aquarius pictures the blessings which follow: the inexhaustible reservoir of water symbolizes the fulness of the renewing, comforting and sanctifying power of His Holy Spirit. *"I will pour out my Spirit upon all flesh; and your sons and daughters shall prophesy, your old men shall dream dreams, your young men shall see visions"* (Joel 2:28). This prophecy, so graphically illustrated by the heavenly water bearer, denotes a physical application to restored Israel; their identity temporarily lost to history, but known to God.

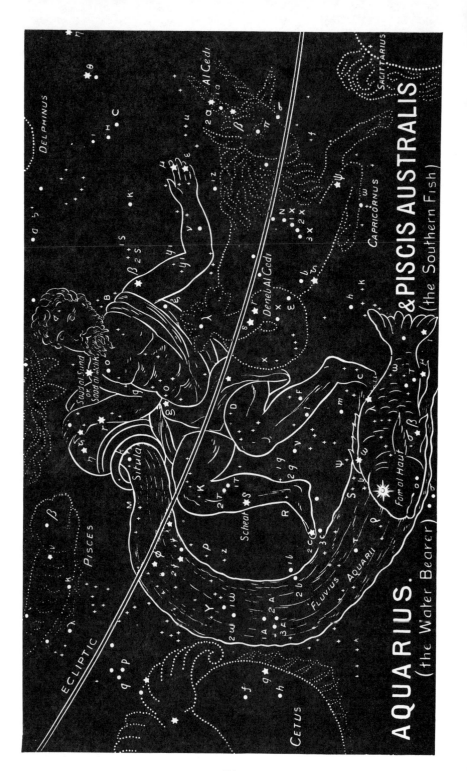

AQUARIUS.
(the Water Bearer)
&PISCIS AUSTRALIS
(the Southern Fish)

Isaiah prophesied of the time when Israel shall be restored, and their eyes shall see their King in His beauty, in these words: *"Fear not O Jacob, my servant; and thou Jesurun, whom I have chosen. For I will pour water upon him that is thirsty, and floods upon the dry ground: I will pour my spirit upon thy seed, and my blessings upon thy offspring"* (Isaiah 44:2-3).

It should be pointed out that Israel is the people to whom Jesus sent His disciples. They were the "Lost Sheep of the House of Israel" who (together with a large portion of the House of Judah that did not go into Babylonian captivity) have been identified by archaeology as the Cimmerians and Scythians. They, in turn, formed the modern Anglo-Saxon, Scandinavian, Germanic, Lombardic and Celtic nations. The House of Israel is today an innumerable multitude apart from Jewry, a fact which the Jewish Chronicle of May 2, 1879 recognized by its reference to the ten lost tribes as represented by peoples who are not Jews.

The Scriptures speak of a future restoration of the House of Israel who were divorced from the Mosaic law, their identity being temporarily lost. They were to be recovenanted, in Christ, to enjoy the Israel birthright through Joseph, a "multitude of nations", in the Isles of the Sea and the land in the wilderness; to be His national evangelists in the world, and the inheritors of the Kingdom of God. The prophets displayed meticulous care when addressing the "House of Israel" or the "House of Judah". To apply a prophecy which refers to one "House" to the other is clearly to misapply the message and confuse the issue. A careful regard of this distinction is prerequisite to the correct understanding of the prophetic Scriptures as well as the symbology of the Zodiac.

Isaiah speaks of the time when Israel will reconstitute the Kingdom of God; *"the glorious Lord will be unto us a place of broad rivers and streams"* (Isaiah 33:21). Ezekiel also foretold Israel's restoration to receive His blessings: *"For I will take you from among the heathen, and gather you out of all countries, and will bring you into your own land"* (Ezek. 36:24). This was in fulfillment of God's covenant with Israel: *"Moreover I will appoint a place for my people Israel, and will plant them, that they may dwell in a place of their own, and move no more, neither shall the children of wickedness afflict them any more, as beforetime"* (II Sam. 7:10). Since the children of Israel were in Palestine at the time of that promise, it follows that the appointed place had to be somewhere other than Palestine. The westward movement of the Israel clans is traced (out of the East-from the land of their Assyrian captivities) by their "waymarks", left behind them, as they journeyed toward their ultimate destinations.

Theologians may scoff at identifying the Western Christian nations as being of ancient Israel but they have no explanation for these peoples who do not know their ancestral origin but who possess all the distinguishing marks of the so-called lost "House of Israel". Eventually they will be found and recognized, not only by themselves, but by the rest of the nations of the earth. Because these were the people of whom God told Hosea to say: *"Ye are not my people and I will not be your God"*, many theologians believe the House of Israel was cut off forever. However, they overlook the further prophecy of Hosea 1:9-10 which states: *"Yet the number of the children of Israel shall be as the sand of the sea, which cannot be measured nor numbered: and it shall come to pass, that in the place where it was said unto them, Ye are not my people, there it shall be said unto them, Ye are the sons of the living God."*

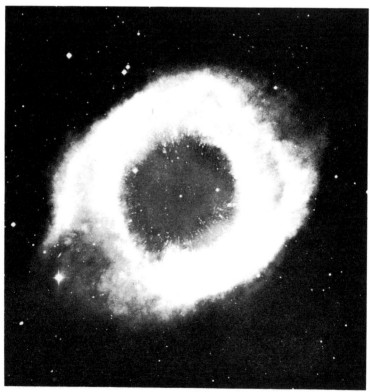

NGC 7293, THE RING NEBULA IN AQUARIUS.

76

1. PICUS AUSTRALIS [the Southern Fish]

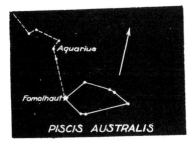

Consists of 23 stars: one of the five of the 4th, etc.

The great fish that receives the flowing water from the urn of the Water Bearer, is known as the "Southern Fish". Its brilliant star of the first magnitude was a subject of much interest by the Egyptians. In the Zodiac of Denderah, this sign was called "Aar", meaning "a stream".

The mythical legends give us little help in regards to the interpretation of this constellation, however, the imagery of this sign and the imagery of the Scriptures record and set forth the same evangelic truth. The redeemed (who were to become a light to lighten the Gentiles, to proclaim His salvation to the ends of the earth—Isaiah 49:6) represented by the mystic fishes, receive the eternal blessedness, symbolized by the waters proceeding from the Fountain (Christ). *"I will open rivers in high places, and fountains in the midst of the valleys: I will make the wilderness a pool of water, and the dry land springs of water"*(Isaiah 41:18). *"...and thou shalt make them drink of the river of thy pleasures. For with thee is the fountain of life."*(Psalms 36:8-9).

PEGASUS (the Winged Horse)

2. PEGASUS [the Winged Horse].

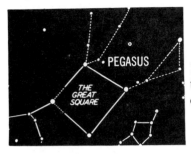

Consists of 89 stars: one of the 1st magnitude: two of the 2nd: three of the 3rd: nine of the 4th, etc.

Here is the figure of a great horse galloping forward with full speed, with great wings spreading from his shoulders. Only the foreparts are shown and the figure is named "Pega" or "Pacha", meaning "the chief". A similarity in names is noted in the Zodiac of Denderah, in which we find two characters immediately below the winged horse, "pe" and "ka". Combining these characters with the letters Sus, meaning "horse", produced the name "Pegasus".

Pegasus is one of the landmarks of the late summer sky. As it appears in the east, the horse seems to be flying almost on its back. The star names of this sign show us that it portrays no mere horse. Its three brightest stars are: Scheat (in the upper right shoulder) meaning "who goeth and returneth"; Markab (marking the beginning of the neck) meaning "returning from afar" and Algeneb (at the lip of the wing) meaning "who carries". The other star-names, indicating the meaning of the picture, are: "Enif", meaning "the branch" and "Homan", meaning "the waters".

The elements of the star-names are consistent with the symbol of Aquarius standing for the Promised Seed, whose word was *"Go ye into all the world and preach the Gospel [Good Tidings of the Kingdom] to every creature. He that believeth and is baptized shall be saved"*(Mark 16:15, 16). The promise of the Holy Spirit, to accompany the spread of the Glad Tidings, was fulfilled on the day Pentecost when *"suddenly there came a sound from heaven as of a rushing mighty wind, and it filled all the house where they were sitting: And they were all filled with the Holy Ghost and began to speak with other tongues, as the Spirit gave them utterance"* (Acts 2:2, 4).

Pegasus was known to the Greeks as the "horse of the gushing fountain". The true Pegasus is Christ who procured blessings for the redeemed by His Atonement, and is coming quickly to pour those blessings upon a famishing world.

CYGNUS (the Swan)

3. CYGNUS [the Swan]

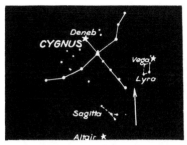

Consists of 81 stars: one of the 2nd magnitude approaching the 1st: six of the 3rd: twelve of the 4th, etc.

This constellation lies in and parallel to the path of the Milky Way. It is the figure of a swan, the lordly king-bird of the waters. The principal stars, marking its wings and length of body, forming a large and beautiful cross, the most perfect of all crosses formed by the constellations. Viewed as a bird, it is flying south,

In classic writings the swan was considered the emblem of poetic dignity, purity and grace. Various legends relate to this sign, which is also called the Northern Cross. It is associated with the swan into which Zeus transformed himself when he was wooing Leda, the wife of the king of Sparta.

In the Zodiac of Denderah, the name of this figure is "Tes-ark", meaning "this from afar". The meaning of this constellation is reflected in its star-names. Its brightest star, Deneb (in the tail) means "the Lord" or "Judge to come". Three of its other more important stars are, in Hebrew, Sadr (in the body) meaning "who returns as in a circle"; Azel (in the tail) meaning "who goes and returns quickly", and Fafage (in the tail) meaning "gloriously shining forth". These star-names continue to picture a risen and glorified Redeemer.

As the white dove is the emblem of the Holy Spirit, so the elegantly pure and graceful swan, bearing the cross, is a fitting emblem of Him who, dying, sends forth the glad river of living waters. *"If any man thirst, let him come unto Me, and drink"* (John 7:37).

In the total zodiacal constellation of Aquarius we have, pictured in the stars, the heavenly waters of life and salvation - the source being the "Seed" of the woman. He, who because of His great love for us, gave His life for our atonement. Resurrected after death, He assumed a new form of brightness and glory in the heavens, assuring us that He will return quickly to bring the waters of everlasting life.

PISCES the Fish and THE BAND

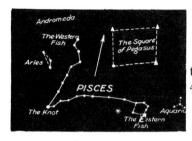

Consists of 113 stars: One of the 3rd magnitude: Eleven of the 4th, etc.

The figures which represent this constellation consist of two large fishes. One is headed toward the North Polar Star, the other is parallel with the path of the Sun. They are some distance apart but are bound together by a Band or ribbon, which is also fastened to the neck of Cetus, the Sea Monster.

The ancient Egyptian name of this constellation, as shown on the Zodiac of Denderah, is "Pi-Cot Orion" or "Pisces Hori", meaning "the fish prolonged", giving the idea of posterity or successive generations. The Hebrew name is "Dagim", meaning, "the fishes". In the Arabic as well as the Greek and Latin names we find the meaning is also "the Fishes".

In the fish shooting upward is pictured the heavenly calling of Israel, and her functioning as His Kingdom, fulfilling its spiritual requirements. The other, keeping on the horizontal, answers to the fact that the Kingdom is established upon the earth and is inheritor not only of the spiritual blessings but of the material blessings and promises made to Abraham and his seed. Being two in number expresses the potential of multitudes, as we find in Gen. 48:16; Jacob blesses the two sons of Joseph, saying: *"Let them grow into a multitude [as "fishes" - marginal note] in the midst of the earth".* This was a continuance of God's covenant with Abraham: *"That in blessing I will bless thee, and in multiplying I will multiply thy seed as the stars of the heaven, and as the sand which is upon the sea shore: and thy seed shall possess the gate of his enemies. And in thy seed [Christ] shall all the nations of the earth be blessed; because thou hast obeyed my voice"* (Gen. 22:17-18)

This seed of Abraham is again referred to, in Psalms 33:12, as *"The nation whose God is the Lord, and the people whom He hath chosen for His own inheritance".* Of this same seed, Isaiah prophesies - *"Their seed shall be known among the Gentiles [nations] and their offspring among the people; all that see them shall acknowledge them, that they are the seed which the Lord hath blessed"*(Isa. 61:9); *"Thou has multiplied the nation, Thou has increased their joy"*(Isa. 9:3 - R.V.).

Ezekiel also wrote concerning this seed: *"I will multiply men upon you, all the house of Israel, even all of it: and the cities shall be inhabited, and the wastes shall be builded: and I will multiply upon you man and beast; and they shall increase and bring fruit"* (Ezek. 36:10, 11).

Fishes also stand as the symbol of the individual believers in Christ. Jesus called and appointed His first ministers and said: "I will make you fishers of men" (Matt. 4:19). In the parable of the drag-net, God's people are again contemplated as fishes. In the Old Testament, fishes also stand for the multitude of people.God told the Israelites, *"Behold, I will send for many fishers, and they shall fish them"* (Jer. 16:16), *"...and there shall be a very great multitude of fish, because these waters shall come thither"* (Ez. 47:9).

The Gospel is likened to a net, which the minister servants of the Lord spread in the waters in order to enclose and gather men - not to destroy them, but to secure them for Himself. When they are thus secured and brought within the enclosure of the influences and laws of the Gospel as Christ's professed followers, they are His mystic fishes, caught by His command and direction and made His peculiar property.

1. THE BAND

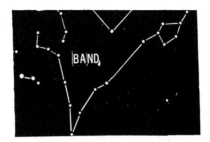

Although the stars in the Band are included in the count of the constellation Pisces, the Band has always formed a separate constellation. Antarah, an Arabian poet of the sixth century, frequently mentions it as distinct from the constellation with which it is closely connected.

The Arabic name of this star group is "Al Risha", meaning "the band" or "bridle". The Egyptians called it "U-or" which means "He cometh". This corresponds to the relationship of the Coming One to His redeemed, *"I drew them with cords of a man, with bands of love: and I was to them as they that take off the yoke on their jaws"* (Hosea 11:4).

The bands that bind the fishes are also fastened to the neck of Cetus, the sea-monster, which shows that Israel is bound and oppressed by the enemies of God. But - her deliverance is near, pictured by the paw of the Ram lying across the doubled part of the band as though about to loosen the bands and set the captives free. Jesus redeemed Israel and set them free from the penalty of the law so that they could again become His people and establish His Kingdom on earth; *"For the Lord hath redeemed Jacob, and ransomed him from the hand of him that was stronger than he"* (Jer. 31:11). Modern Israel (of which America is a part) is still bound politically, economically and ecclesiastically).

The next of the minor constellations of Pisces also tells the story of captive Israel (Andromeda) chained and afflicted.

ANDROMEDA
(the Chained Woman)

2. ANDROMEDA [the Chained Woman]

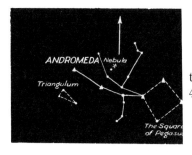

Consists of 63 stars: three of the 2nd magnitude: twelve of the 4th, etc.

This is a picture of a beautiful woman, with chains fastened to her feet and arms in such a manner that she is unable to rise. The stars that form this figure are well suited to the image of a chained woman for they curve out in a long line, like the links of a chain or the knots in a cord, from the Milky Way to the corner of the Great Square of Pegasus. Even when the maiden was not recognized, the idea of bonds persisted; the Arabs pictured a Seal, chained by the neck to the fainter line of stars underneath it.

In the Denderah Zodiac the woman is named "Set", which means "set, set up as a queen". In Hebrew she is "Sirra", "the chained". The brightest star (in her head) is called in Arabic, "Al Phiratz" meaning "the broken down". Other stars and their meanings are: Mirach (Hebrew), "the weak"; Al Anak (Arabic), "struck down"; Mizar, "the weak"; Al Mara, "the afflicted".

Thus all the stars in this constellation speak to us of Israel today, a captive daughter of Zion, bound and fettered (economically and spiritually) waiting for the Coming One for deliverance from her enemies who encompass her within and without. *"Shake thyself from the dust; arise and sit down O Jerusalem; loose thyself from the bands of thy neck, O captive daughter of Zion. For thus saith the Lord, Ye have sold yourself for nought; and ye shall be redeemed without money"* (Isaiah 52:2, 3).
"The virgin daughter of My people is broken with a great breach, with a grievous blow" (Jer. 14:17).

Classic mythology, surrounding Andromeda, has obscured but failed to fully hide the symbology of this sign. The fables say that she was the daughter of Cepheus and Cassiopeia, promised to her uncle (Phineus) in marriage, when Neptune sent a flood and a sea-monster to ravage the country. This was in answer to the resentful clamors of his favorite nymphs against Cassiopeia

87

because she boasted herself fairer than Juno and the Nereides. Nor would the incensed god be pacified until, at the instance of Jupiter Ammon, the beautiful Andromeda was exposed to the sea-monster, chained to a rock near Joppa in Palestine, and left to be devoured. But Perseus, on returning from the conquest of the Gorgons, rescued her and made her his bride.

The stars of Andromeda were also known in Chaldea centuries before Greek and Roman legends. There, she was known as the "Chained Maiden" and the destruction of Cetus, the sea-monster by Perseus was paralleled in their story of Marduk and the dragon Tiamat. The myth of the hero who slays a vile monster, usually to win the hand of a fair maiden, is one of the oldest and most common in mythology and fairy tales. It is basically the same story. One can only conclude, such stories have a common origin; the most ancient being this Celestial portrayal of the Chained Woman.

We have no great difficulty in recognizing Israel (Christian nations of today) as the beautiful Andromeda. Although redeemed at Calvary, she is surrounded by world power, jealous of her material blessings, who hate her and threaten her destruction. But, there is One who is engaged in a war with the children of darkness who plot the woman's death. Presently, He will come to rescue and deliver the fair maiden, to make her His own glorious bride. This "bride" will be dealt with, more fully, in the constellation of Cassiopeia.

M31, THE GREAT SPIRAL GALAXY IN ANDROMEDA

3. CEPHEUS [a Crowned King]

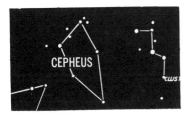

Consists of 35 stars: three of the 3rd magnitude: seven of the 4th, etc.

Here is a presentation of a crowned king wearing his royal robe and enthroned in the highest heaven. He bears aloft a sceptre and his foot is over the Pole-star. His Greek name "Cepheus" is from the Hebrew and means "the branch". His Ethiopian name is "Hyk", meaning "a king". In the Zodiac of Denderah, the figure in this sign is a large front leg of an animal connected with a small figure of a sheep, in the same posture as Aries in the next constellation. The Egyptians called this sign "Pe-ku-hor", which means, "this one cometh to rule".

CEPHEUS (the Crowned King)

If there was ever any doubt as to the meaning of this constellation it is dispelled by the meanings of the star-names that make up this sign. The brightest star (in the right shoulder) is called "Al Deramin" which means "coming quickly". The next brightest star (in the girdle) is named, in Arabic, "Al Phirk", meaning "the Redeemer". The third brightest star (in the left knee) is called "Al Rai", meaning "who bruises" or "breaks".

When we consider what the Scriptures tell us of the exultation and glory of Jesus Christ, it is impossible to mistake the truth which these star-names teach. Christ has been invested with all royal rights and dominion. It was predicted of Him *"He shall bear the glory, and shall sit and rule upon His throne"* (Zech. 6:13) *"Which he wrought in Christ, when he raised him from the dead, and set him at his right hand in the heavenly places, Far above all principality, and power, and might, and dominion, and every name that is named, not only in this world, but also in that which is to come:"* (Ephesians 1:20, 21).

In Cepheus, we have the glorious King of Israel. It is He who calls Israel His son. To Moses He said, as recorded in Exod. 4:22: *"Thus saith the Lord, Israel is my son, even my first born"*.

In the thirty-third chapter of Jeremiah, after speaking of Israel's restoration, God says: *"At the same time, saith the Lord, will I be the God of all the families of Israel, and they shall be my people...for I am a father to Israel, and Ephraim is my firstborn"*. Here is the foundation of Israel's blessing. Not yet fully made manifest, but as "the Lord reigneth", He will in due time make good His word, for, *"The counsel of the Lord standeth forever, the thoughts of his heart to all generations. Blessed is the nation whose God is the Lord, and the people whom he hath chosen for his own inheritance"* (Psalms 33:11, 12).

CHAPTER VIII – CONSTELLATION ARIES

[the Ram or Lamb]

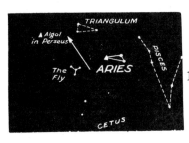

Consists of 66 stars: one of the
1st magnitude: two of the 4th, etc.

The figure in this constellation is that of a vigorous Ram or
Lamb. It's Hebrew name is "Taleh" meaning "the Lamb". The
Arabic name is "Al Hamal", "the sheep, the merciful, the gentle".
In Syrian it was called "Amroo", "the Lamb", the same as John
1:29 where it says, *"Behold the Lamb of God, which taketh away
the sin of the world".* The ancient Akkadians called this figure,
"Baraziggar", "Bar", meaning "altar" or "sacrifice", "Ziggar",
meaning, "right making"; so that the full name would mean, "the
sacrifice of righteousness".

To the Egyptians (by the time of the Eighteenth Dynasty)
Aries represented Amon, the supreme sun-god, king of all the
gods, and they portrayed him as a man with the head of a ram. In
the Zodiac of Denderah, however, they picture Aries as a lamb
without horns, and crowned with a circle and is called "Tamelouris
Amon," which means, "the reign, dominion" or "government of
Amon".

Its chief star (in the forehead) is named "El Nath" or "El
Natik", which means "wounded, slain". The next brightest star (in
the left horn) is "Al Sheratan", meaning "the bruised" or "the
wounded". In the year of the Crucifixion of Jesus, the chief star of
this constellation shown overhead, at the noonday darkening of the
sun, on the day the Lamb of God was slain.

The mythical stories concerning Aries further identify him
with the Lamb of God. This mysterious lamb was given by nephele
to her two children, Phrixus and Helle, when Ino, their mortal
stepmother was about to have them sacrificed to Jupiter. It was by
seating themselves on the lambs back and clinging to its fleece that
the children were able to make their escape. These two children,
(as did the two fishes) symbolize Israel. Under sentence of death,
Israel was redeemed by the blood of the *"Lamb of God, which
taketh away the sin of the world"* (John 1:29).

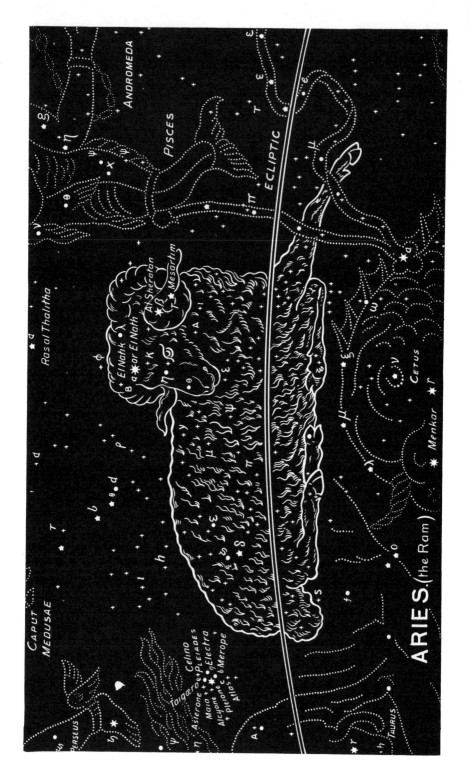

ARIES.(the Ram)

Nephele's Lamb was sacrificed to Jupiter in place of those who were saved by him; so Christ, the true Aries, was sacrificed for us, and died in our stead. *"Worthy is the Lamb that was slain to receive power and riches, and wisdom, and strength, and honour, and glory and blessing"* (Rev. 5:12).

Some ancient pictures of this constellation show a triangle over the head of the Lamb, which the Greeks said exhibited the name of the Deity it was supposed to represent. This explanation can only be indicative of a truth once known but lost; the mystery of the Trinity (God in three Persons). This truth was evidently make known to our ancient fathers and foretold in the constellation Aries.

The Egyptians celebrated a sacred feast to the Ram upon the entrance of the Sun into the sign of Aries. They prepared for it before the full moon next to the spring equinox, and on the fourteenth day of that moon all Egypt was in joy over the dominion of the Ram. The ancient Persians had a similar festival of Aries. It is hard to account for these traditional legends except in connection with what was prophetically signified by Aries. But taken in relation to what the Scriptures foretell of the Lamb, in the period when He shall take to Him His great power for the establishment of His kingdom on earth, we can easily see how this would come to be one of the very gladdest and most exultant of the sacred feasts. It is when the Lamb thus comes upon the throne, the gladdest period in all the history of the people of God is come.

1. CASSIOPEIA [the Enthroned Woman]

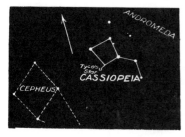

Consists of 55 stars: five of the 3rd magnitude: five of the 4th, etc.

Here we see the figure of a queenly woman, matchless in beauty, seated in exalted dignity. In one hand she holds aloft the branch of victory and triumph, and with the other she is spreading and arranging her hair as if preparing for some great public manifestation.

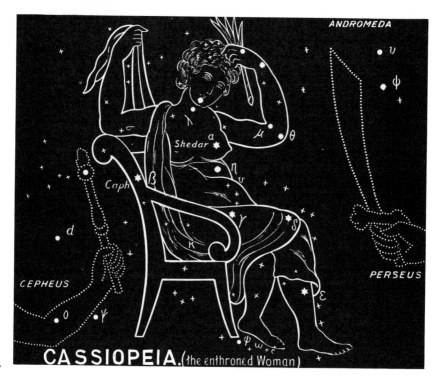

CASSIOPEIA. (the enthroned Woman)

The Arabic name for this constellation is "El Seder"; "the freed". Its Chaldee name "Dat al cursa", means "the enthroned". In the Denderah Zodaic her name is "Set", which means "set up as Queen". Four stars of the third magnitude, which never set, form the seat upon which this woman sits. The brightest star (in the left breast) is "Schedir", which, in Hebrew, means "the freed". The next brightest (in the top of the chair) is "Caph" (also Hebrew), meaning "the branch", probably derived from the branch of victory which she bears in her hand.

Although Cassiopeia is universally represented as the mother of Andromeda, the woman bound; it is self evident that she is the same woman, freed, delivered and enthroned. Seated upon the Artic circle, and close by the side of Cepheus, the King, she portrays the Biblical picture of restored Israel, the Bride of the Lamb, who addresses her thus: *"For thy Maker is thine husband; the Lord of hosts is his name; and thy Redeemer the Holy One of Israel; The God of the whole earth shall he be called. For the Lord hath called thee as a woman forsaken and grieved in spirit, and a wife of youth, when thou wast refused, saith thy God. For a small moment have I forsaken thee: but with great mercies will I gather thee. In a little wrath I hid my face from thee for a moment; but with everlasting kindness will I have mercy on thee, saith the Lord thy Redeemer".* (Isaiah 54: 5-8).

Some theologians, today, teach that the "Church" (all true believers) is to become the "Bride of Christ". In doing so, they wrongly interpret Ephesians 5:25 where Christ's love to His Church is only COMPARED to a husband's love for his wife. On the contrary, it reveals the secret that the Church of Christ is to be the mystical "Body of Christ", part of the Husband in fact, *"One new man* (Eph. 2:15). *"And hath put all things under his feet, and gave him to be head over all things to the church* ("Ecclesia" or "called out ones"): *Which is his body, the fulness of him that filleth all in all"* (Eph 1:22). *"And he is the head of the body, the church: who is the beginning, the first born from the dead; that in all things he might have pre-eminence"* (Col 1:18).

The Old Testament clearly identifies restored Israel to be the Bride of this "New Man"; the Lamb's wife. *"...as a bridegroom decketh himself with ornaments, and as a bride adorneth herself with her jewels...*(Isa. 61:10). Psalms also identifies Israel (Queen) as the Bride: *"The King's daughter is all glorious within: her clothing is of wrought gold. She shall be brought unto the king in raiment of needlework: the virgins her companions that follow her shall be brought unto thee. With gladness and rejoicing shall they be brought: they shall enter into the king's palace"* (Psalms 45: 13-15).

95

2. CETUS [the Sea Monster]

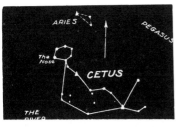

Consists of 97 stars: two of the 2nd magnitude: eight of the 3rd: nine of the 4th, etc.

This largest of all the constellations depicts a vast scaly beast with an enormous head, mouth and front paws, possessing the body and tail of a whale. It is considered an animal of the waters and the natural enemy and devourer of fishes. This great sea-monster is the true "Leviathan" of Job and Isaiah. The Creator asks Job: *"Canst thou draw out leviathan with an hook? or his tongue with a cord which thou lettest down? Canst thou put an hook into his nose? or bore his jaw through with a thorn?* (Job 41:1, 2).

In the Denderah Zodiac it is pictured as a monstrous head, trodden under foot by the swine (a natural enemy of the serpent) and named "Knem", meaning "subdued". The hawk, another enemy of the serpent, is over this figure, crowned with a mortar denoting "bruising".

The brightest star (in the upper jaw) is named "Menkar"; the "bound" and "chained" enemy. The next in brightness (in the tail) is called "Diphda" or "Deneb Kaitos"; "overthrown" or "thrust down". Another star (in the neck) is named "Mira", which means "the Rebel". Mira is a variable star. From a magnitude of two it disappears periodically seven times in six years.

Fastened to the neck of this monster is the Band which holds the Fishes (Israel) after passing the front foot or hand of the Lamb. Clearly, this constellation is a striking symbol of the Devil, or Satan (the great Rebel whom Israel cannot bind) holding Israel bound and oppressed. We find, in the sign of Cetus a foreshadowing of how the enthroned Lamb will bind and punish Leviathan, even as the written word of prophecy describes: *"For, behold, the Lord cometh out of his place to punish the inhabitants of the earth for their iniquity: the earth also shall disclose her blood, and shall no more cover her slain. In that day the Lord with his sore and great and strong sword shall punish Leviathan the piercing serpent, even Leviathan that crooked serpent; and he shall slay the dragon that is in the sea"* (Isaiah 26:21 - 27:1).

PERSEUS (the Breaker)

3. PERSEUS [the Breaker]

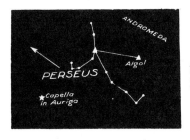

Consists of 59 stars: two of the 2nd magnitude: four of the 3rd: twelve of the 4th, etc.

Here is the figure of a mighty man, stepping with one foot on the brightest part of the Milky Way, wearing a helmet on his head and wings on his feet. In his right hand he holds aloft a great sword and in his left hand he is carrying away the blood dripping head of an enemy he has slain. The man's Hebrew name is "Peretz" from which we get the Greek form, "Perses" or Perseus", meaning "the Breaker". The same title is used of Christ in Micah 2:13: *"The breaker is come up before them; they have broken up, and have passed through the gate, and are gone out by it; and their king shall pass before them, and the Lord on the head of them".*

In the Denderah Zodiac the man is called "Kar Knem","he who fights and subdues". The head, which the breaker carries, is called by the Greeks the head of "Medusa" which is obviously a perversion since the Hebrew rendering the name means: "the trodden under foot". Another Hebrew name for the head is "Rosh Satan", "the head of the adversary". In Arabic we have the name "Al Oneh", or "Al Ghoul", meaning "the subdued", or "the evil spirit".

The star names of this constellation bear witness to the interpretation of the picture. The major star (in the waist) is named "Mirfak"; "who helps". Another star (in the right shoulder) is called, "Al Genib"; "who carries away". A bright star (in the left foot) is called, "Athik" which means, "who breaks".

'Perseus is perhaps one of the best loved and admired of all the hero-gods of mythology. He was the son of the divine Father, who went forth against the three Gorgons; those horrible fabled creatures with bodies indissolubly together and covered with impenetrable scales. Their heads were full of serpents in place of hair and they had the power to turn to stone any one on whom they fixed their gaze. To equip Perseus for his expedition, Pluto lent him his helmet, which had the power of rendering the wearer invisible. Minerva furnished him with her buckler, resplendent as a polished mirror, and Mercury gave him wings for his feet and a diamond sword for his hand. Thus outfitted, he mounted into the air, led by the goddess of wisdom, and came upon the tangled monsters. Severing the head of Medusa, the only one of the three Gorgons subject to mortality, he returned to be made immortal and take his place among the stars, ever holding fast the reeking head of the Gorgon. It was on his return from this brave deed that he saw the beautiful Andromeda chained to the rock, and the terrible monster of the sea advancing to devour her. On condition that she should become his wife, he broke her chains. He then plunged his sword into the monster that sought her life, fought off and turned to stone the tyrant Phineus who sought to prevent the wedding, and made Andromeda his bride. By varied miracles he changed portions of the earth, its governments and rulers. From time to time Perseus returned to bless the countries that honored him.

In the light of the revelation of the previous sign it is impossible to mistake the truth hidden in this mythical legend. The Greeks, though they had lost the true meaning of the legend, perserved a trace of it, even in their perversion of it. No natural events in the history of man adequately account for the existence of such a story except the story of the Seed of the woman, begotten of the Father, who became the Lamb that was slain, thereby destroying the power of the Serpent. Girded with divine wisdom and splendor He "breaks" the way of His people as He leads His people westward to their "appointed place". There-having lost their identity, they sat as Andromeda, helpless in their own strength despised, hated, threatened by the serpents of Medusa's head and exposed to the attacks of the monster lord of this world.

Foretold in the constellation of Perseus is the coming time when He who walks amid the golden candlesticks and holds in His hand the seven stars will lift up the title-deed of their inheritance and reveal His lost people Israel, while He destroys all His enemies, putting Leviathan in bonds. Then He will raise Andromeda to Cassiopeia's throne as His bride.

CHAPTER IX — CONSTELLATION TAURUS [the Bull]

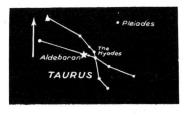

Consists of 141 stars: One of the 1st magnitude: one of the 2nd: three of the 3rd, etc.

The figure of this constellation is the head and broad shoulders of a Bull, rushing forward with mighty energy, with his sharp star-pointed horns set to push his enemies and pierce them through and destroy them. In all the ancient Zodiacs the Bull is shown in the act of pushing or rushing. The Denderah Zodiac terms this sign "Isis", meaning "who saves" or "delivers"; and "Apis", meaning "the head" or "chief". The names of this sign in Hebrew, Syriac, Arabic, Latin and Greek mean the same as the English name, "The Bull".

For thousands of years the Egyptians worshipped a bull-god, Apis. This Apis was no shadowy figure in a shadowy heaven but a living animal, a bull in whose form the divine Osiris was thought to be incarnated. He was called "Osiris-Apis", known in classical times as "Serapis". The bull was worshipped by the Chaldeans as the god of spring, symbol of the young sun. To the Summerians, he was the "Bull of Light" who kept the cycle of the seasons spinning in the sky and so brought each in turn to the earth, bringing springtime again after winter's death. He was the sacred bull that must be sacrificed by the god Mithra before the sun could rise. He was the Cretan Minotaur, hidden in the labyrinth of stars. All these bulls seem to be descended from the original bull of the heavens; Taurus the star-bull.

The most conspicuous stars in Taurus are the Hyades, a cluster of stars which form its face. This clear V-shaped star group was "Al Debaran" (in the bulls eye), meaning "the leader" or "captain" (Chaldee). Another major star (at the tip of the left horn) is in Arabic, "El Nath", meaning "wounded" or "slain". In the neck of Taurus is another cluster of stars called the "Pleides" (the Seven Sisters). The word means "the congregation of the judges" or "rulers". The brightest star in this group is "Al Cyone" (Arabic), which means, "the center". Some leading astronomers believe it is the center of the universe. apparently that is what was implied when Job is asked of God, *"Canst thou bind the sweet influences of Pleiades?"* (Job 38:31).

THE OPEN CLUSTER OF THE PLEIADES,

In Taurus we have a prophecy of Christ, the coming Judge, Ruler, and "Lord of all the earth". To His own He is the "Lamb", but toward the unsanctified world He finally becomes the irresistible Lord of Judgment on God's great day of Judgment. Speaking of that day, the Holy Spirit says by Isaiah: *"For the indignation of the Lord is upon all nations, and his fury upon all their armies: he hath utterly destroyed them, he had delivered them to the slaughter". "For it is the day of the Lord's vengeance, and the year of recompences for the controversy of Zion".* (Isaiah 34: 2,8).

It should be pointed out that the judgment time, called the "Day of Judgment", is not limited to a period of twenty-four hours; it is rather a period of time of judgment such as that which is spoken of as, *"the day that the Lord God made the earth and the heavens"* (Gen 2:4).
when we read the sign of Taurus we see the foreknowledge of the day when the Lord, who is very long-suffering now, will reach the limit of His forebearance to sin added upon sin and wickedness upon wickedness. There is a time coming when He will come to execute judgment on the earth. The Scriptures tell us how *"the Lord Jesus shall be revealed from heaven with His mighty angels. In flaming fire taking vengeance on them that know not God, and that obey not the Gospel of our Lord Jesus Christ"* (II Thess. 1:7-8).

The first of the minor constellations continues the prophecy of a coming judge; to show that the Coming One is no mere Bull, but a man: a mighty, triumphant and glorious prince.

ORION
(the Glorious One)

1. ORION [the Coming Prince]

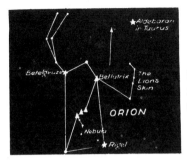

Consists of 78 stars: two of the 1st magnitude: four of the 2nd: four of the 3rd: sixteen of the 4th, etc.

Orion is the most brilliant of all the constellations. The figure contained therein is a great hunter with a mighty club in his right hand shown in the act of striking. In his left hand he holds the skin of a slain lion. His left foot is in the act of crushing the head of the enemy. He wears a brilliant starry girdle from which hangs a mighty sword. The hilt of the sword is in the form of the head and body of a lamb; showing the mighty prince is "the Lamb that was slain".

In Greek and Roman mythology, the figure of Orion was the center of many legends concerning the hero-god who lived and died on earth, but even then he had been no ordinary man. He was a giant in stature and courage; a great hunter who had the power to walk unharmed over the waters of the earth. His death came about because of the anger of Juno over hearing him boast, one day, that there was no animal on earth he feared. She determined he should die the most humiliating death she could devise for him. She then sent a scorpion to sting his heel, and the great hunter, the son of the sea-god, (Neptune) was fatally wounded by the poison of the creature.

That such fables reflect the pure image of Christ can be clearly perceived. Christ was born of a woman, as was alleged of Orion. He was, at the same time, the peculiar gift of Deity to our world, as was the hero of the constellation. Christ was indeed the greatest and sublimest of all men. He passed through water without being wetted. He did claim to be able to destroy, and came into the world that He might destroy all the mighty powers of evil and all the works of the Devil. On this account He was stung by the Scorpion of death.

The names of the stars in this sign substantiate this interpretation. The brightest star (in the right shoulder) is named

105

"Betelgeuz"; "the coming of the branch". The next in brilliancy (in the left foot) is called "Rigel" or "Rigol"; "the foot that crusheth". The lifted foot in the very act of crushing the head of the enemy thus illustrates the name. Another star (one of the three in his belt) is called "Al Nitch"; "the wounded One" and reminds us of the prophecy that this glorious One was to be bruised in the heel. In His left breast shines a bright star, "Bellatrix", which means "swiftly coming" or "suddenly destroying". Other star-names (Arabic) relate to this prince. Al Giauza; "The branch"; Al Gebor, "the mighty"; Al Mirzaim, "the ruler", Al Nagjed, "the prince", Niphla, (Chaldee) "the might"; Nux (Hebrew), "the strong".

Again we see the foreknowledge that the Prince of Glory, who was once wounded for the sins of His people, is about to rise up and shine forth for their deliverance. Their redemption draweth nigh: for *"The Lord shall go forth as a mighty man, he shall stir up jealouy like a man of war: he shall cry, yea, roar; he shall prevail against his enemies. I have long time holden my peace; I have been still, and refrained myself: now will I cry like a travailing woman: I will destroy and devour at once"* (Isaiah 42:13-14).

In that day we shall see the beauty and glory of the truth revealed: *"Arise, shine: for thy light is come, and the glory of the Lord is risen upon thee. For behold, the darkness shall cover the earth, and gross darkness the people: but the Lord shall arise upon thee, and his glory shall be seen upon thee. And the Gentiles [nations] shall come to thy light, and kings to the brightness of thy rising"* Isaiah 60: 1-3).

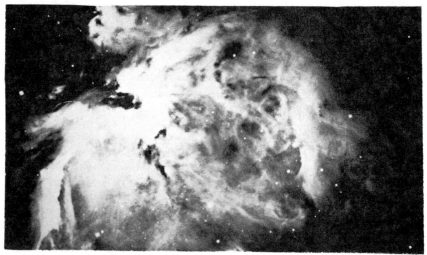

THE GREAT NEBULA OF ORION.

2. ERIDANUS]The River of the Judge]

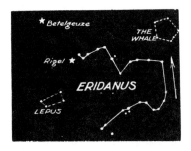

Consists of 84 stars; one of the 1st magnitude; one of the 2nd; eight of the 3rd; etc.

Here we have an immense river flowing forth from before the glorious Orion, running in a serpentine course toward the lower regions. In vain, the sea monster Cetus strives to stop its flow. In the Denderah Zodiac, it is a river under the feet of Orion. Its name is given as "Peh-la-t", which means "the mouth of the river".

The brightest star (at the mouth of the river) is named "Achernar", which is in (as its name indicates) "the after part of the river". The next star (in the source of the river) is "Cursa", which means "bent down". Other stars are "Zourac" (Arabic); "flowing"; "Pheat"; "mouth"; and "Ozha"; "the going forth".

In Daniel's vision of the four beasts, and God's judgment of them, we find this same "River of the Judge": *"I beheld till the thrones were cast down, and the Ancient of days did sit, whose garments were white as snow and the hair of his head like the pure wool. His throne was like a fiery flame, and his wheels as burning fire. A fiery stream issued and came forth from before him; ...the judgment was set and the books were opened"* (Dan. 7: 9-10).

This sign speaks of judgment, associated with fire, as does the Greeks myths concerning this sign. Though grossly perverted, they still connect it with fire. According to their fables, something went wrong with the chariot of the sun and a universal conflagration was threatened. In the trouble "Phaeton" was killed and hurled into this river, in which he was consumed by fire. The whole earth was affected from the burning heat.

This same picture is presented in the Psalms: *"Our God shall come, and shall not keep silence: a fire shall devour before him, and it shall be very tempestuous round about him"* (Psalms 50: 3). *"A fire goeth before him, and burneth up his enemies round about. His lightenings enlightened the world: the earth saw, and trembled. The hills melted like wax at the presence of the Lord, at*

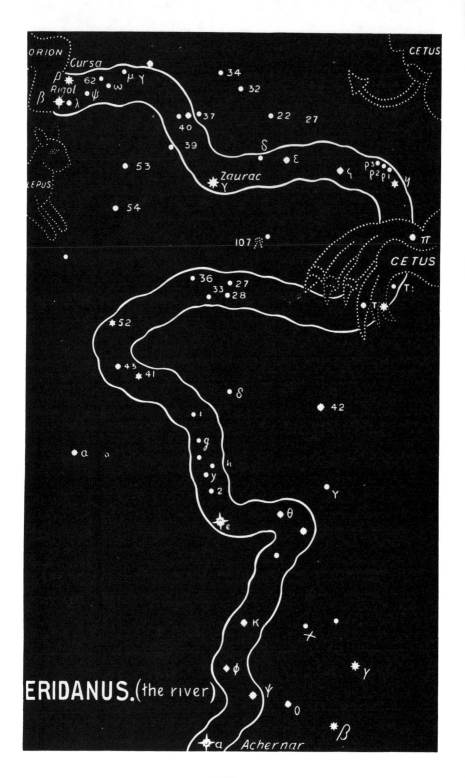

ERIDANUS. (the river)

the presence of the Lord of the whole earth" (Psalms 97: 3-6).

Also, we read in Isaiah: *"Behold, the name of the Lord cometh from far, burning with his anger, and the burden thereof is heavy; his lips are full of indignation, and his tongue as a devouring fire...and the Lord shall cause his glorious voice to be heard, and shall shew the lighting down of his arm, with the indignation of his anger, and with the flame of a devouring fire, with scattering and tempest, and hailstones"* (Isaiah 30: 27-30).

Again in Nahum, we find: *"The mountains quake at him, and the hills melt and the earth is burned at his presence, yea the world, and all that dwell therein. Who can stand before his indignation? and who can abide in the fierceness of his anger? his fury is poured out like fire, and the rocks are thrown down by him"* (Nahum 1:5-6).

There is, however, mercy in judgment. Although the present church-age will have ended before the promised Seed of the woman takes on the character described in this chapter, probation will not have entirely ended. The possibility of securing salvation will not yet have been completely cut-off. *"Many shall be purified, and made white, and tried; but the wicked shall do wickedly, and none of the wicked shall understand; but the wise shall understand* (Dan 12:8-10). Seemingly, many who have lost all chance of reaching the first honors of the kingdom will come through judgment to embrace that remaining opportunity. Hence Isaiah prophesied: *"When Thy judgments are in the earth, the inhabitants of the world will learn righteousness"* (Isaiah 26:29). So also the Psalmist says: When God shall shoot His arrows at them that encourage themselves in evil, and shall suddenly wound them, *"men shall fear, and declare the work of God; for they shall wisely consider His doing"* (Psalms 64:7-9). And again; *"Thy people shall be willing in the day of Thy power"* (Psalms 110:3).

Apparently, in the day of judgment, the wicked shall not understand, seeing as Paul says, *"That because they receive not the love of truth, God sendeth them a working of error, that they may believe a lie, and be irremediably condemned"* (II Thes. 2: 10-12).

These are very awesome and terrifying presentations, but they are true pictures, exactly the same, both in the Scriptures and in the constellations. They are given as a warning to a sinful, careless and indifferent world. There is, however, one escape from the wrath to come, and that way is given in the next sign.

3. AURIGA]the Shepherd]

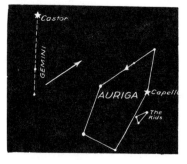

Consists of 66 stars: one of the 1st magnitude; two of the 2nd; nine of the 4th, etc.

Here we see a Great Shepherd, seated on the Milky Way, holding a she-goat on his left arm. She is looking down frightened at the terrible rushing bull. On the man's lap are two frightened little kids, apparently just born, and trembling with fear. The Greeks called the man, "Haeniochos", which in their language signified a "Driver" or "Charioteer". This tradition resulted in our modern atlases calling him the "Wagoner". In Latin, the word "Auriga" means a "coachman" or "charioteer", although the name "Auriga" is from a Hebrew root which means "a shepherd".

The brightest star (in the body of the goat) is named "Alioth" (Hebrew) which means "a she-goat". Its modern Latin name "Capella" has the same meaning. The next star in brightness (in the shepherd's right arm) is called "Menkilinon" and means "the band" or "chain of the goats". Another bright star (in his right foot) is called "El Nath" which bears the significant and revealing meaning - "wounded" or "slain". Yet another star is "Maaz" which means "a flock of goats".

The Greek myths are totally at a loss to explain this sign, although they preserved the traditional figure. Yet these stars were familiar as far back as there is any echo of astronomy. In all the Aryan and Mediterranean lands they were always depicted in the same strange way, a vague and somewhat crooked kite. Even at that, the kite is made up only by borrowing one star - El Nath - that properly belongs to Taurus. Nevertheless, the constellation has always been described as a man driving a chariot, with the reins gathered up in his hands. There is no chariot and no horse, but always he holds his reins ready and always he carries the goat and its little family.

It has been suggested that the goat might have been a later addition, due to some confusing of words, such as that which

110

AURIGA (the Shepherd)

turned the seven bears of India into seven saints, but the figure is too old for that. The constellation existed in the same form, goat and all, in the earliest Chaldee astronomy. If one could penetrate a little further into earlier mythology, unrecorded and now forgotten, we would find the explanation of the strange figure who has gathered up a goat and her kids, in the story of the Good Shepherd who laid down His life for the sheep. *"Therefore I will save my flock, and they shall no more be a prey"* (Ezek. 34:22). What is depicted as "reins" in the hands of the shepherd is actually the same "bands" that once bound Israel; loosened by the hand of the Lamb; now held by the Good Shepherd for evermore. Foretold in Auriga is a glorious coming of an exalted and almighty Saviour.

111

In that day of wrath and judgment *"He shall feed his flock like a shepherd: he shall gather the lambs with his arm, and carry them in his bosom, and shall gently lead those that are with young"* (Isaiah 40:11). *"Come unto me, all ye that labour and are heavy laden, and I will give you rest"* (Matt. 11:28). *"But the salvation of the righteous is of the Lord: he is their strength in the time of trouble. And the Lord shall help them and deliver them...from the wicked, and save them, because they trust in him"* (Psalms 37: 39, 40).

In the Zodiac of Denderah, the same truth was revealed more than 4000 years ago; but the man figure, instead of carrying sheep, is carrying a sceptre with the head of a goat, its end, under his hand, forms a cross. The Egyptians knew nothing of the death on the cross, having lost the true message of the Zodiac - retaining only the cross as a sign of eternal life.

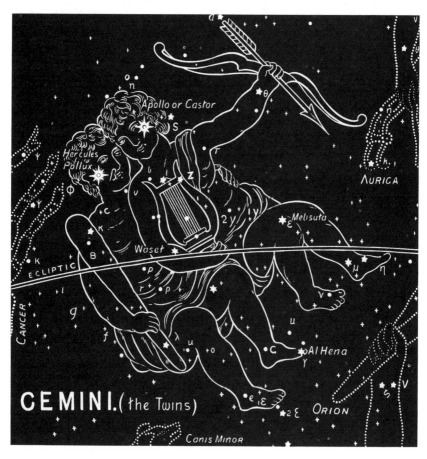

GEMINI. (the Twins)

CHAPTER X — CONSTELLATION GEMINI [the Twins]

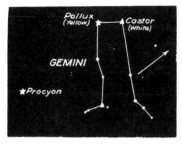

Consists of 85 stars: two of the 2nd magnitude: four of the 3rd: nine of the 4th, etc.

Gemini pictures two youthful-looking figures walking or coming. Some atlases show them seated. One holds a great club in his right hand, while the other figure holds a harp in one hand and a bow and arrow in the other. Both the club and the bow and arrow are in repose, the same as the figures which hold them.

The Latins called the figures "Castro" and "Pollux", although the Greeks claimed to have invented them, and they called them "Apollo" and "Hercules", the sons of Jupiter. The Coptics called them "Pi-Mahi", "the united", as in brotherhood, or "the completely joined". The Hebrew name for this sign is "Thaumin" which means, "united".

In the Zodiac of Denderah the figure is that of a man walking hand in hand with a woman. The man has an appendage (Hor, or Horus) which signifies "the Coming One". Having identified the masculine figure, there can be no difficulty in identifying the accompanying female figure as the bride (Israel) of the Lamb. When we closely examine the names still retained in this constellation, we find ample indication that the figures were meant to set forth Christ and His bride (Israel) in a yet further great marriage-union at the close of this present world order when Christ's blessings will fall upon restored Israel. In His love and mercy these blessings are offered to all who acknowledge Him as their Saviour and King.

The name of the principal star (in the head of the figure that holds the club) is called " Pollux " , which means "ruler" or "judge". Another star (in his left foot) is called "Al Henah", which means "hurt, wounded", or "afflicted". In the center of his body is another bright star, called "Wasat", which means "Set, Seated", or "Put in place", as where it is said in the Scriptures; "I am SET on the throne of Israel", "There are SET thrones of judgment", "the judgment was SET", "I am SET in my ward".

The Scriptures proclaim: *"Behold, the days come, saith the Lord, that I will raise unto David a righteous Branch, and a King shall rein and prosper, and shall execute judgment and justice in the earth. In his days Judah shall be saved, and Israel shall dwell safely: and this is his name whereby he shall be called, THE LORD OUR RIGHTEOUSNESS"* (Jer. 23:5, 6). *"Behold, the days come, saith the Lord, that I will perform that good thing which I have promised unto the house of Israel and to the house of Judah. In those days, and at that time, will I cause the Branch of righteousness to grow up unto David: and he shall execute judgment and righteousness in the land'*(Jer. 33: 14, 15).

This is what we see pictured in the constellation Gemini; Messiah's peaceful reign. All is rest and repose after a great victory gained. We see "His days," in which *"the righteous shall flourish; and "abundance of peace, so long as the moon endureth"* (Psalms 72:7). The accompanying minor signs of Gemini tell us that before this eternal kingdom is come, the earth must be delivered from misrule and oppression. All enemies must be subdued.

LEPUS.(the Hare) or ENEMY

1. LEPUS [the Hare]

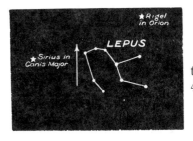

Consists of 19 stars: three of the 3rd magnitude: seven of the 4th, etc. ☐

The figure of a hare has no relationship with the ancient names of the stars making up this constellation. As is also the case with the other two minor constellations of Gemini. All three carry Latin names indicative of more or less modern origin. Although the Arabic called the figure "Arnebeth", which means "the Hare", to learn its real meaning we must refer to the more ancient zodiacs. The Persians pictured it as a serpent while to the Egyptians (Denderah Zodiac) it is an unclean bird standing on the serpent which is under the downtrodden foot of Orion. Its name, there, is given as "Bashti - beki". Bashti meaning "confounded" and "Beki" meaning "failing".

The brightest star (in the body) has a Hebrew name, "Arnebo", which means the enemy of Him that cometh". The Arabic name "Arnebeth" means the same. Other stars included in this sign are in Arabic: "Nibal","the mad"; "Rakis", "the bound"; "Sugia", "the deceiver".

From these indications there can be no mistaking the Hare as the enemy whom the true Orion shall destroy as it is written: *"And ye shall tread down the wicked; for they shall be ashes under the soles of your feet in the day that I shall do this; saith the Lord of hosts"* (Mal. 4:3) and *"for he it is that shall tread down our enemies"* (Psalms 60:12).

Isaiah also prophesies of that day: *"I will tread them in mine anger, and trample them in my fury...For the day of vengeance is in mine heart, and the year of my redeemed is come"* (Isaiah 63:3, 4).

2. CANIS MAJOR [the Dog]

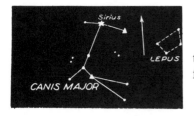

Consists of 64 stars: two of the 1st magnitude: two of the 2nd: four of the 3rd: four of the 4th, etc.

Modern zodiacs carry the picture of a great dog, which has its origin in Greek mythology. The Egyptians pictured it as a hawk or eagle, and called it "Apes", which means, "the head". The hawk is the natural enemy of the serpent, and here it has on its head a pestle and mortar, indicating the fact that he shall crush the head of the enemy. The Persian Zodiac pictured it as a wolf and called it "Zeeb", meaning "leader". In Hebrew it has the same meaning, while in Arabic it means "coming quickly".

CANIS MAJOR (the Dog)

The names of the stars of this constellation have no meaning whatever as applied to an Egyptian hawk or with a Greek dog. But they are full of meaning when applied to Him of whom Isaiah speaks: *"Behold, I have given him for a witness to the people, a leader and commander to the people"* (Isaiah 55:4).

The brightest star (in the head) and the brightest in the whole heavens, is called "Sirius" (from Sir, or Seir) meaning "Prince, Guardian, the Victorious". Though this "Dog-Star", as it came to be known, was associated with burning heat, pestilence and disaster to the earth, it was not so in more ancient times. In the ancient Akkadian it was called "Kasista", which means, "the Leader". The second star (on the left forefoot) is named "Mirzam" and means "the prince " or "ruler". A star (in the body) is called "Wesen", meaning "the bright, the shining". Another star (in the right hand leg) is named "Adhara", meaning "the glorious".

Other stars have similar meanings: "Aschere" (Hebrew), "who shall come"; "Al Shira Al Femeniya" (Arabic), "the Prince" or "chief of the right hand"; "Seir" (Egyptian), "the Prince"; "Abur" (Hebrew), "the mighty"; "Al Habor" (Arabic), "the mighty"; "Muliphen" (Arabic), "the leader, the chief".

A significant prophetic note can be found in the star Sirius, which is derived from Seir". Taken in connection with the name of the figure in the Egyptian Zodiac, as often given, we have "Naz-Seir" or "Nazer"; "Naz-Seir", meaning "the Sent Prince". According to the Scriptures, the "Rod" promised to come forth from the stem or stump of Jesse is called "Netzer" in the Hebrew Bible. There, it is translated "the Branch" who should "smite the earth with the rod of His mouth, and slay the wicked with the breath of His lips". Jesus spent His earlier years at an obscure little village by the name of "Nazareth". Thus, all the star-names harmoniously weave a consistent and magnificent picture of the "Sent Prince"; the "Branch"; the "Netzer" of Isaiah; the "Naz-seir-ene" of the prophetic constellations, and the "Nazarene" spoken of by the prophets (Matt. 2:23).

3. CANIS MINOR [the Second Dog].

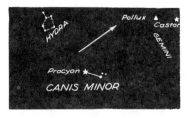

Consists of 14 stars: one of the 1st magnitude: one of the 2nd: one of the 4th, etc.

This constellation, as in the case of the preceeding sign, reveals nothing by its picture or its name. To obtain its original meaning we must search the ancient zodiacs and the names of the stars which have come down to us. In the Denderah Zodiac the sign is represented as a human figure with a hawk's head and the appendage of a tail. The figure is called "Sebak" which means, "conquering, victorious". Arabic astronomy designated the figure as the "Prince of the left hand".

The brightest star (in the body) is named "Procyon", which means "Redeemer". The next star (in the neck) is called "Al Gomeisa" (Arabic) meaning "the burdened, loaded down" or "enduring for the sake of others". Other star-names and their meanings are: "Al Mirzan", "the prince" or "ruler"; "Al Gomeyra", "who completes" or "perfects"; "Al Shira" or "Al Shemeliya" (Arabic), "the prince" or "chief of the left hand".

Here there is no conflicting voice; no discord in the harmonious testimony to Him, whose name is called *"Wonderful, Counsellor, the Mighty God...the Prince of Peace"* (Isaiah 9:6). Despite the perversion of the picture of this and the preceeding sign, their stars carry the primeval message - the Coming One. Canis Major, indicative of His triumphant return, Canis Minor portraying His return as our Redeemer.

CANIS MINOR
(the second Dog)

CHAPTER XI—CONSTELLATION CANCER [the Crab].

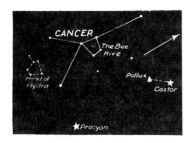

Consists of 83 stars: one of the 3rd magnitude: seven of the 4th, etc.

This constellation is one of the faintest in the sky, and certainly it is the most insignificant group of stars placed in the Zodiac. Having no stars more than the third magnitude, it is practically impossible to view, unless atmospheric conditions are very good.

In our modern zodiacs we have the picture of a gigantic Crab. It is the same in the Hindoo and Chinese Zodiacs. Here again, it is evident that the original picture, as well as those of Cancer's first and second minor constellations, has been lost, because they do not agree with the meaning of their star-names. The Denderah Zodiac however provides us with the key to its meaning. Although portrayed as a sacred beetle, Cancer was called "Klaria", meaning "the folds, the resting places". This is in perfect harmony with all its star-names, as well as the minor constellations and their star-names. In other Egyptian zodiacs, it is represented by the head of an eagle, which is probably Cancer's original picture.

This is borne out by the Arabic name for the sign which is "Al Sartan", which means "who holds" or "binds". The Syrian name "Sartano" means the same. The Greeks called it "Karkinos" which means "holding" or "encircling" as does the Latin, "Cancer" and hence applied to the crab.

The brightest star (in the tail) is called "Tegmine", which means, "holding". Another star (in the lower large claw) is called "Acubene". The Psalmist wrote: *"He that dwelleth in the secret place of the Most High shall abide under the shadow of the Almighty"* (Psalm 91:1). God said of Israel, *"Ye have seen what I did unto the Egyptians, and how I bare you on eagle's wings, and brought you unto myself"* (Exod. 19:4).

In the center, nearly overshadowing this constellation, is one of the brightest nebulous clusters in the starry sky, and sufficiently luminous to be seen with the naked eye. It is made up

CANCER. (the Crab)

of a multitude of little stars, and is called, by modern astronomy, the "Bee-hive". The ancients called it "Praesepe", which in its Arabic and Hebrew elements, means "The multitude, offspring, the Innumerable Seed".

This same meaning is repeated in another star; Ma'alaph" (Arabic) which means "assembled thousands". To Israel are added a *"great multitude", which no man could number"* gathered with them before the Throne and before the Lamb (Rev. 7:9). That the "multitudes" represent Israel protected by the Good Shepherd is shown to us by the name of another star; "Al Hamarein" (Arabic) which means "the kids" or "lambs".

1. URSA MINOR [the Little Bear]

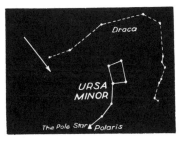

Consists of 24 stars: one of the 2nd magnitude: two of the 3rd: four of the 4th, etc.

Here again we come to an ignorant Greek perversion of primitive truth. No bear ever existed with such a long uplifted tail as is shown on modern atlases of the constellations. No traces of a bear is to be found in Chaldean, Egyptian, Persian or Indian Zodiacs. Possibly, Ursa Minor (as well as Ursa Major) came to be called "Bears" because the ancient name of the principal star in Ursa Major is "Dubhe" or "Dubah" which is similar to "Dob" the word for Bear. However, Dubhe or Dubah does not mean bear, but a collection of domestic animals, a "fold".

In Arabic, "Dubah" means "cattle". In Hebrew, "Dohver" is a "fold" and "Dohveh" means "rest and security". The same word occurs in Duet. 33:25, *"As thy days so shall thy strength be"*. The Revised Version gives in the margin, *"So shall thy rest or security be"*. This interpretation is fully corroborated in the meaning of the star-names making up this sign.

One bright star is named "Kochab" which means, "waiting Him who cometh". Other star-names and their meanings are: "Al Pherkadian" (Arabic) which means "the calves" or "the young" (as in Deut. 22:6); "the redeemed assembly"; "Arcas" or "Arctos", "a travelling company" and according to one interpreter, "the stronghold of the saved". This "Lessor Sheepfold" (Ursa Minor) could well represent the smaller company, the "little flock" that Christ mysteriously transfers (as the Church of the first born) to heaven, prior to His return, to become His "body".

The most important star in the whole heavens and the major star of this constellation is named "Al Ruccaba", which means "the turned" or "ridden on". It is today known as the "Polar" or "North Star" This central star does not appear to revolve in a circle as does every other star. At the time when the constellations were mapped (approximately 7000 years ago) the Dragon Star (Alpha Draconis) was the Pole Star which marked the central gate or hinge of the earth's motion. But, by its gradual recession the Dragon Star is now far away from the Pole, while the Lesser Sheepfold has come into its place, so that the main star Al Ruccaba is now the Pole Star.

Thus prophetically, in Ursa Minor we find a picture of the old prophecy fulfilled, when Satan is cast down and Israel is to *"possess the gate of his enemies"* [Gen. 22: 17] - that is, hold what the enemy previously held. *If there is any doubt that Divine Inspiration named the stars, consider the name of the present Polar Star - "Al Ruccaba", meaning, "the turned" or "ridden on". What man by his own powers, some 7000 years ago could have known that this star would someday be literally the turning point of the heavens?*

2. URSA MAJOR [the Great Bear]

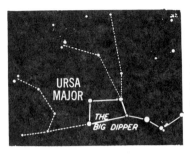

Consists of 87 stars: one of the 1st magnitude: four of the 2nd: three of the 3rd: ten of the 4th, etc.

This constellation is one of the best known of all the heavenly constellations. Its seven major stars, so well matched in brightness and so conspicuous as a group, are very well known as the "Big Dipper" or "Plough" (Britain). The handle of the Dipper (three stars) is in the tail of the Bear, and the other four stars, forming the bowl, lie in the hind part of the body. As in the case of the preceeding constellation, we are dependent upon the ancient star-names for the true meaning of this sign.

The brightest star (in the back) is called "Dubhe", meaning "a herd of animals" or "a flock" and gives its name to the whole constellation. A similar meaning is found in the old Arab name for the constellation, "Al Naish" or "Annaish", meaning "assembled together" as sheep in a fold. The next important star (in the center of the body) is named "Merach", which means in Hebrew, "the flock" and in Arabic "purchased". Another star (in the middle of the so-called tail) is called "Mizar", meaning "separate" or "small" and close to it is "Al Cor" meaning "the Lamb". A star (at the end of the tail) is named "Benet Naish" (Arabic) meaning "the daughters of the assembly". It is sometimes called "Al Kaid", "the assembled".

Other star-names and their meanings are: "El Alcola" (Arabic), "the sheepfold" (as in Psalms 95:7, 100:3); "Cab'd al Asad","multitude, many assembled"; "Annaish", "the assembled"; "El Kaphrah", "protected, covered" (Hebrew), "redeemed" or "ransomed"; "Dubheh Lachar" (Arabic), "the latter herd" or "flock"; "Helike", "company of travellers"; "Amaza" (Greek), "coming and going"; "Calisto", "the sheepfold set" or "appointed".

Again, no evidence of a "bear" is indicated by the meaning of the star-names. The indications are that according to the original intent, we are to see in the two constellations (Ursa Minor and Ursa Major) not two long tailed bears but two "sheepfolds" or

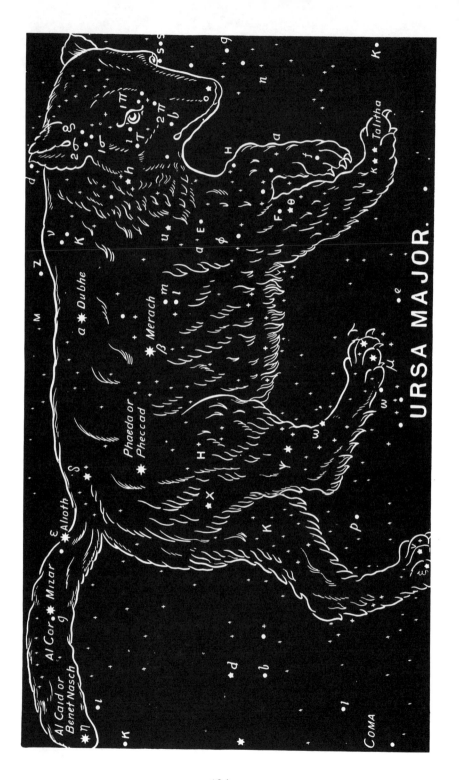

URSA MAJOR.

"folded sheep": One the lesser (Ursa Minor) and one the greater (Ursa Major). With this idea in mind, a glance will show that the seven stars (Little Dipper) in the Little Bear and the seven stars (Big Dipper) in the Great Bear answer to an enclosure, from which the flocks go forth from the fold, at the corner, led by their great Shepherd and Guardian. All the stars testify to the same fact that His sheep are to be gathered into the fold:

It is written as plainly in the Scriptures as it is in the heavens: *"As a shepherd seeketh out his flock in the day that he is among his sheep that are scattered; so will I seek out my sheep, and will deliver them out of all places where they have been scattered in the cloudy and dark day. And I will bring them out from the people, and gather them from the countries, and I will bring them to their own land, and feed them upon the mountains of Israel by the rivers and in all the inhabited places of the country. I will feed them in a good pasture, and upon the high mountains of Israel shall their fold be:there shall they lie in a good fold, and in a fat pasture shall they feed upon the mountains of Israel."* (Ezek. 34:12-14).

"The Lord hath appeared of old [or from afar] unto me, saying, Yea, I have loved thee with an everlasting love: therefore with loving-kindness have I drawn thee. Again I will build thee, and thou shalt be built, O virgin of Israel:"...Hear the word of the Lord, O ye nations, and declare it in the isles afar off, and say, He that scattered Israel will gather him, and keep him, as a shepherd doth his flock"* (Jer. 31:3, 4, 11).

In contradiction to the prevailing religious teachings that declare that because God has caused Israel to be driven from the land of Palestine, He had cast them away forever, we find God is faithful and has kept His Everlasting Covenant made with Abraham and his descendants, Israel. This began with the fall of the Assyrian Empire when portions of the exiled tribes started westward across Europe toward the Isles in the Sea. From our history, traditions and "marks" it can be shown that the United States of America is characteristic of the tribe of Manassah, although peopled by a gathering of all the tribes of Israel.

ARCO. (the Ship)

3. ARGO [the Ship]

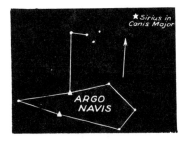

Consists of 64 stars: one of the 1st magnitude: six of the 2nd: nine of the 3rd: nine of the 4th, etc.

This is the mythical ship of the mighty Argonauts of which Homer sang nearly ten centuries before Christ. Many and varied are the suggestions to explain it. Some think that Noah's Ark gave birth to the story and the picture, but the evidence points to the prophetic rather than a record of the past. Whatever fables have gathered round the story of this ship, there is no doubt regarding its antiquity.

It is clear that when divested of mythic details, the ancient sailors after all their experiences, came home victorious. The Golden Fleece, for which they went in search, tells of a treasure that had been lost. Jason, the captain, tells of Him who recovered it from the Serpent which guarded it with ever-watchful eyes. Is this not the parable of the hidden treasure (the Lost Sheep of the House of Israel) hidden in the field of the world; found by the Good Shepherd, who then went and sold all that He had and bought it with His Blood?

It is a large vessel, as indicated by the immense size of the constellation, as well as the large number of its stars. Its name "Argo" means "company of travellers"; *"a great multitude which no man can number"* (Rev. 7:9), harmonizes with the star-names. The brightest star (near the keel) is named "Canopus" or "Canobus", which means "the possession of Him who cometh". Other star-names are: "Sephina", meaning "the multitude" or "abundance";"Tureis","the possession";"Asmidiska","the released who travel"; "Soheil" (Arabic), "the desired"; and "Subilon", "the Branch".

This same thought is expressed in the words of Jeremiah: *"Therefore fear thou not, O my servant Jacob, saith the Lord; neither be dismayed, O Israel: for lo, I will save thee from afar, and thy seed from the land of their captivity; and Jacob shall return, and shall be in rest, and be quiet, and none shall make him afraid. For I am with thee, saith the Lord, to save thee...''(Jer. 30:10, 11).*

In the Denderah Zodiac we find Argo pictured as the figure of a great ox enclosed, with the cross suspended from his neck. This would symbolize a great possession, marked with the ancient token of immortality and eternal life. The name of the figure is "Shes-en-Fent", which means, "rejoicing over the Serpent". Although having a different picture, it expresses the same Scriptural promises; the safe folding of His blood-bought flock into a kingdom of everlasting rest.

Isaiah sings: *"The ransomed of the Lord shall return, and come to Zion with songs and everlasting joy upon their heads: they shall obtain joy and gladness, and sorrow and sighing shall flee away"*(Isaiah 25:10). John in prophetic vision looked over into that other age, and writes: *"They shall hunger no more, neither thirst any more; neither shall the sun light on them, nor any heat. For the Lamb shall feed them, and shall lead them unto living fountains of waters: and God shall wipe away all tears from their eyes. (Rev. 7:16,17). "And there shall be no more death, neither shall there be any more pain: for the former things are passed away"*(Rev. 21:4).

Jesus says: *"To him that overcometh will I grant to set with Me in my throne, even as I also overcame and am set down with my Father in His throne"*·(Rev. 3:21). These are promises that shall surely be fulfilled. God has pledged Himself by His oath to make them good. They are the same that glowed in the hearts of the primeval patriarchs, who saw them afar off, and were persuaded of them, and embraced them. On the imperishable stars they hung and pictured their confident belief and anticipation, whereby they, being dead, could speak - speak across these many thousands of years - speak for our comfort, on whom the end of the age has come.

CHAPTER XII—CONSTELLATION LEO [The Lion]

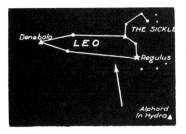

Consists of 95 stars: two of the 1st magnitude: two of the 2nd: six of the 3rd: thirteen of the 4th, etc.

There is no confusion about this sign. In all the ancient zodiacs of Egypt and India, as well as modern ones, we find a great Lion in all the majesty of His fierce wrath. His feet are over the head of Hydra, the great serpent, and just about to descend upon it and crush it. The Hebrew name of the sign is "Arieh", which means "the Lion". There are six Hebrew words for Lion, and the one used is of a Lion "hunting down his prey". The Syrian name is "Aryo", meaning "the rendering Lion", while the Arabic name is "Al Asad", meaning "a lion coming vehemently".

In the Denderah Zodiac the Lion is treading upon a serpent and its name is "Pi Mentekeon", which means "the poured out". The hieroglyphics beneath the Lion read "Knem", meaning "who conquers" or "is conquered", referring to the victory over the serpent. The truth of this sign is self-evident to any student of the Bible. The "Lion of the tribe of Judah" aroused for the rendering of the prey.

In the prophecy of Balaam we read: *"He shall eat up the nations his enemies, and shall break their bones, and pierce them through with his arrows, He couched, he lay down as a lion, and as a great lion, who shall stir him up?"* (Num. 24:8, 9). Isaiah describes the scene: *"The Lord shall go forth as a mighty man, he shall stir up jealousy like a man of war: he shall cry, yea, roar; he shall prevail against his enemies"* (Isaiah 42:13). This is what was meant when John, the Revelator, was told *"...the Lion of the tribe of Judah, the Root of David, hath prevailed to open the book..."* (Rev. 5:5) and *"Worthy is the Lamb that was slain to receive power, and riches, and wisdom, and strength, and honour, and glory, and blessing"* (Rev. 5:12).

All the stars in Leo magnify and exalt Him as the Coming Conqueror and Judge: The brightest star (on the Ecliptic) is called "Regulus", meaning "treading under foot" . Because it marks the heart of the Lion it is sometimes called by its modern name "Cor

Leonis", which means, "the heart of the Lion". The next star (in the tip of the tail), also the 1st magnitude, is named "Denebola", meaning, "the Judge" or "Lord who cometh". The next star (in the mane) is called "Al Giebha" (Arabic) meaning, "the exaltation". Another star (on the hind part of the back) is called "Zosma", which means "shining forth".

Other star-names and their meanings are: "Sarcam" (Hebrew), "the joining" (intimating that here is the point where the two ends of the Zodiacal circle have their joining); "Minchir al Asad" (Arabic), "the punishing" or "tearing of the Lion"; "Deneb Aleced", "the judge cometh who seizes"; "Al Dafera" (Arabic), "the enemy put down".

As nearly and fully as names can express it, we have the same things in the Zodiacal Leo that we find ascribed to the Lion of the tribe of Judah in the Apocalypse. They both tell one and the same story - the story of the wrath of the Lamb and His great final judgment - administrations, in which the mystic "Stone" Kingdom (Book of Daniel) cut out of the mountain without hands, falls upon, breaks in pieces all other kingdoms and powers. Zephaniah also prophesies of that day; *"Therefore wait ye upon me, saith the Lord, until the day that I rise up to the prey: for my determination is to gather the nations, that I may assemble the kingdoms, to pour upon them my indignation, even all my fierce anger: for the earth shall be devoured with the fire of my jealousy"* (Zeph. 3:8).

Even among the stupendous works of battle and judgment, as He exercises the powers and prerogatives of the Lion, Christ never ceases to be the Lamb of God. By His sacrificial death and mediation, His people have achieved their redemption. He is the Lion to His enemies and to His friends, the Lamb - "slain from the foundation of the world". By His blood the saints are washed from their sins, their garmets made white, and their final victory over all Satan's accusations assured.

Such is the Lion-work of the "Root" and "Offspring of David" as it was revealed to the Apostle John and directed to be written for our learning. What is thus pictured in the last book of the Scriptures is the same that was fore-ordained and recorded in this last sign of the Zodiac, before any book of our present Bible was written. In the three minor constellations of this sign, the work of Leo is more fully developed and described.

HYDRA (the Serpent) CRATER (the Cup) CORVUS (the Raven)

1. HYDRA [the Serpent]

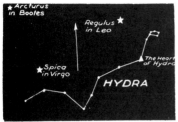

Consists of 60 stars: one of the 2nd magnitude: three of the 3rd: twelve of the 4th, etc.

Pictured here is an immense female serpent, whose length stretches one-third the way around the whole sphere of the heavens; Its uplifted head near the Little Dog Star and its tail pointing at Libra. Crater and Corvus lie on its back, side by side. The name "Hydra" means "the Abhorred" (The Fleeing).

The brightest star (in the heart of the Serpent) is called "Al Phard" (Arabic) which means "the separated, put away". The next star is named "Al Drian", meaning "the Abhorred". Another star is "Minchar al Sugia", meaning "the piercing of the deceiver".

According to the myths, this Hydra was the terrible water snake which answers to the picture of *"the Great Dragon, that old Serpent, called the Devil and Satan, which deceiveth the whole world"*(Rev. 12:9). His Satanic kingdom, over which he reigns and which he inspires and directs as another god against Almighty God, has set itself against the establishment of God's kingdom in earth as it is in heaven" (Matt 6:10).

Satan, once a good angel and a chief among the angels, "kept not his first estate", but abused his free will to sin and rebel. He seduced our first parents into transgression; not as a literal serpent, but as a visible, treacherous, intelligent, evil spirit, who reappears again and again in the history and prophecies of the Scriptures. The great mission of the promised Seed of the Woman was to bruise effectually the Serpent's head. This is the all-comprehensive burden of the promise given to the fallen Adam and his children after him.

The two remaining minor constellations of Leo picture the fate of the great deceiver and all who are ensnared into the Serpent's program to destroy God's people Israel and hinder the establishment of His kingdom on earth.

2. CRATER [the Cup]

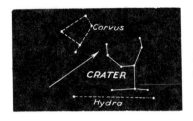

Consists of 13 stars: one of the 3rd magnitude: four of the 4th, etc.

Here is pictured a cup, broad, deep, full to the brim, and placed directly on the body of Hydra, the serpent. The two stars that determine the bottom of the Cup form part of the body of the serpent, indicating it is inseparable from the monster.

This is no fabled wine-cup of Bacchus; but it is, *"the cup of his indignation"* (Rev. 14:10); *"the cup of the wine of the fierceness of his wrath"* (Rev. 16:19). The Psalmist says: *"Upon the wicked he shall rain snares, fire and brimstone, and an horrible tempest: this shall be the portion of their cup"* (Psalm 11:6), *"For in the hand of the Lord there is a cup, and the wine is red: it is full of mixture: and he poureth out of the same; but the dregs thereof, all the wicked of the earth shall wring them out, and drink them"* (Psalm 75:8).

This Cup of divine indignation is the portion of the worshippers of the son of perdition, which is poured out without adulteration or dilution. Dreadful beyond understanding is the picture John, the Revelator, gives of this Cup of unmingled and eternal wrath, but no more dreadful than the picture of it which the primeval prophets have thus inscribed upon the stars.

3. CORVUS [the Raven]

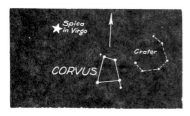

Consists of 9 stars: four of the 3rd magnitude: one of the 4th, etc.

Our final picture is of a raven, the bird of prey, grasping the body of Hydra, the serpent, with its feet and tearing the serpent's body with its beak. Its Hebrew name is "Areb", "the raven". The Egyptians called it "Her-na", meaning "the Enemy broken".

Every star-name in this sign protends judgment and destruction. The brightest star (in the eye) is called "Al Chibar", meaning "the Curse inflicted". The next star (in the right wing) is named "Al Goreb (Arabic), from the Hebrew "Orel", "the Raven". A third star is named "Minchar al Gorab", which means "the Raven tearing to pieces".

The Scriptures often associate birds of prey with judgment and punishment: *"The eye that mocketh at his father, and despiseth to obey his mother, the ravens of the valley shall pick it out, and the young eagles shall eat it"* (Prov. 30:17). When David, the first great impersonation of Judah's Lion, met the terrible Goliath, he cursed him in the name of the Lord, God of Israel, and said: *"I will smite thee, and take thine head from thee; and I will give the carcases of the host of the Philistines this day unto the fowls of the air and to the wild beasts of the earth"* (I Sam. 17:46). In Revelation, the birds are summoned to gather for the task of clearing away the carnage in the final scene of slaughter that accompanies the coming of Him who is "King of Kings" and "Lord of Lords" (Rev. 19: 17-18).

When the Serpent-enemy falls, the circle of time is complete and it is eternity. Satan's grasp upon our world has held through the long succession of two-thirds of the signs. Hardly had Adam received his Divine commission than Satan began schemes to get Adam's posterity in his power and sway them through his will. Through their carnal passions he has perverted their holy worship into idolatries. He has plied them with visions of empire and dominion which have filled the earth with tyranny, misrule, oppressive wars, and political abominations. He has corrupted the thinking and philosophies of men, thereby making them willing slaves to damning error. Even today, he is the very god of this world to whose lies the vast majority of the world render homage.

On the face of the lovely stars it has been written from the beginning, the same as in the Book. Satan's doom is sealed. The Lion he cannot destroy. Satan's power will soon be seized by the Almighty power. The father of lies will be crushed, torn, pierced and forced to drink of the cup of eternal wrath, while the multi-headed body in which he has operated through all the ages is given to the birds of prey to be devoured.

THE HEAVEN'S DECLARE

We began with Virgo and we ended with Leo - and found the ORIGIN and PURPOSE of the Zodiac. There can be no question but that the Gospel glows in these heavenly constellations with all the luster of the stars themselves. God has been, all through the ages, proclaiming from the starry sky the glories, sufferings, triumphs of the Virgin's Child. Can we close our eyes to the testament of the Stars? To do so, is to go against the laws of evidence. Can there be any doubt but that the Zodiac is a primeval fountain of Divine Truth? If there is, it is against the principles of logic.

The Zodiac is primeval "Bible Astrology" (symbology of astronomy); the earliest revelation to mankind from his Creator. Satan perverted God's Astrology, substituting in its place a mythological system designed to control the entire world through fortune-telling, sorcery and witchcraft. "Horoscopic Astrology" speaks of mysterious influences which emanate from "the houses of heavens" (which relate to the Signs of the Zodiac), affecting earthly creatures either favorable or adversely, depending upon how man relates himself to those strange forces. "Biblical Astrology", on the contrary, has nothing at all to say about forces influencing your destiny. It is simply the telling of the Gospel of Jesus Christ through the names which God gave the stars. "Biblical Astrology" proclaims the story of the One, whose self-given Name is "the Light of the World", who dwelt in the midst of the twelve tribes of Israel that they might "behold His Glory".

Knowledge of this Light leads men into the *"paths of righteousness'* - *"Lest ye corrupt yourselves...and lest thou lift up thine eyes unto heaven, and when thou seest the sun, and the moon, and the stars, even all the host of heaven, shouldest be driven to worship them, and serve them, which the Lord Thy God hath divided to all nations under the whole heaven'*(Deut. 4: 16, 19).

It is evident that after the original meaning of the constellations became lost, nations invented stories from their imaginations. The Greek mythology is an erroneous interpretation of the signs after their true meaning had been forgotten. The heathen, in their blindness, could not understand the celestial story and did not know what to make of the foreshowing. But, in the light of God's fuller revelation found in the Scriptures, we read the origin and meaning of it all.

As we read the names of the stars, beginning with Virgo, the Virgin, and learn of "the Seed" and "the Branch", and compare Scripture with Scripture where these names are found, we find the signs of the Zodiac (Mazzaroth) with their related constellations and individual stars preach the Gospel of Christ. These are the "holy prophets" spoken of by Zacharias: *"Blessed be the Lord God of Israel; for he hath visited and redeemed his people. And hath raised up an horn of salvation for us in the house of his servant David; As he spake by the mouth of his HOLY PROPHETS, which have been SINCE THE WORLD BEGAN"* (Luke 1:68-70). Only the star-messengers of God, created and named in the day that God made the heavens and the earth, the constellations of the Zodiac, fit that description.

Our God is a God who knew the end from the beginning. He laid out the perfect plan before He created a single thing. He pictorially inscribed it in the everlasting stars from the beginning. This perfect Plan included and determined all of the events of history, in the most minute detail, with one central purpose - to reveal His Glory, in Jesus Christ.

Agnostics have long offered virgin-born saviours, messiahs, or sons of god, preceeding the Christian era, as criticism of the orthodox Christian position. Such claims are no longer valid in the light of Celestial Revelation. All world religions do show a common origin (by similarities) but it only proves that in the beginning all man-kind was given God's Plan for humanity. In such case, having foreknowledge of a virgin-born saviour, it was no problem for corrupt priests to fabricate one and every ancient religion did just that. Nor did such practices cease with the birth of Jesus Christ because He said: *"Take heed that no man deceive you. For many shall come in my name, saying I am Christ; and shall deceive many"* (Matt. 24:4, 5).

In spite of its confusion and conflicting doctrines, only in Christianity can be found the fountain (fundamental idea) of the "Gospel of the Stars". Ancient religions may imitate crucified saviours - modern religions may corrupt the words of the Book, but neither can touch the stars in the heavens that DO DECLARE, the Glory of God, as embodied in the person - mission - work and redemptive achievements of His only begotten Son, Jesus Christ.

"When I consider Thy heavens"

SUMMARY

CHAPTERS I-IV: THE REDEEMER PROMISED

I - VIRGO:
1. The Seed of the Woman;
2. The Desire of nations;
3. The Man of double nature in humiliation;
4. The exalted Shepherd and Harvester.

II - LIBRA:
1. The Price to be paid;
2. The Cross to be endured;
3. The Victim slain;
4. The Crown purchased.

III - SCORPIO:
1. The Conflict;
2. The Serpents coils;
3. The struggle with the Enemy;
4. The toiling Vanquisher of evil.

IV - SAGITTARIUS:
1. The doubled-natured One triumphing as a Warrior;
2. He gladdens the Heavens;
3. He builds the fires of punishment;
4. He casts down the Dragon.

CHAPTERS V - VIII: THE REDEEMER'S PEOPLE

V - CAPRICORNUS:
1. Life out of Death;
2. The arrow of God;
3. Pierced and falling;
4. Springing up again in abundant life.

VI - AQUARIUS:
1. Life-waters from on high;
2. Drinking in the heavenly flood;
3. Carrying and speeding the Good News;
4. Bearing aloft the Cross over all the earth.

VII - PISCES:
1. Multiplication of the Redeemer's People;
2. Upheld and governed by the Lamb;
3. The intended Bride bound and exposed on earth;

4. The Bridegroom exalted.

VII - ARIES:
1. The Lamb found worthy;
2. The Bride released and making ready;
3. Satan bound;
4. The Breaker triumphing.

CHAPTERS IX- XII: THE REDEMPTION COMPLETED

IX - TAURUS:
1. The invincible Ruler come;
2. The sublime Vanquisher;
3. The River of Judgment;
4. The all-ruling Shepherd.

X - GEMINI:
1. The Marriage of the Lamb;
2. The Enemy trodden down;
3. The Prince coming in Glory;
4. His princely following.

XI - CANCER:
1. The Possession secured;
2. Lesser fold - the Church of the first born; the rulers;
3. Greater fold - Israel, the Bride;
4. Safe folding;into a kingdom of everlasting protection.

XII - LEO:
1. The King aroused for the rending;
2. The Serpent fleeing;
3. The Bowl of Wrath upon him;
4. His carcass devoured.

The whole story is complete. The mystic essence of primeval astrology (astronomy) is the same that constitutes the essence of all that is written by inspiration in the Books of the Bible. There is nothing added and there is nothing left out. The glorious stars take on a holier brightness as the sublime underwriters of our Scriptures. As God's witnesses from beyond the gulf of ages they assure us there is no mistake in building on Jesus of Nazareth as our hope and our salvation. We have considered the "hosts of heaven" and have found them flaming from end to end, from center to circumference, with that superlative "glory of God" which shines "in the face of Jesus Christ." (II Cor. 4:6).

OLD ENGLISH CALENDAR

Aquarius

January and Aquarius

Pisces

February and Pisces

Aries

March and Aries

Taurus

April and Taurus

Gemini

May and Gemini

Cancer

June and Cancer

Leo

July and Leo

Virgo

August and Virgo

Libra

September and Libra

Scorpio

October and Scorpio

Sagittarius

November and Sagittarius

Capricorn

December and Capricorn

A GALAXIE OF STARS

He spread the stars across the universe,
To shine like diamonds in a vaulted hall.
He broadcast them as hand sown seeds might fall
Or as coins spilled out of some rich kings purse.
He then, made man for better or for worse
And placed him on a tiny spinning ball
That whirled around one of the stars so small.
Yet I have heard man give to Him the curse.
Would man in his own adoration bask,
Denying God performed this mighty task
Oh yes, we have these hands - this brain of ours,
And these are free with no restraining bars.
But lest you be conceited with your powers,
Man, make for me a Galaxie of Stars.

© **John Hall**

ACKNOWLEDGEMENT

It is hoped this treatise will suffice to answer those that throw contempt on Christianity as a mere accommodation of certain old mythic ideas, common to all primitive peoples, or a religion reconstructed from oriental systems of worship containing essentially the same basic doctrines as Christianity.

The ideas expressed in this compilation are based on the investigations and studies, "Primeval Astronomy" by Joseph A. Seis D.D., L.L.D. (Gospel of the Stars - 1884) and the further studies of E.W. Bullinger, D.D. (The Witness of the Stars - 1893). Both, in turn, are indebted to the works of Frances Rolleston of Britian (Mazzaroth: or the Constellations - 1875) who performed the drudgery of collecting the compilations presented by Albumazer, the Arab astronomer of the Caliphs of Grendad, 850 A.D. and the Tables drawn up by Ulugh Beigh, the Tartar prince and astronomer, about 1450 A.D., who gives the Arabian Astronomy as it had come down from the earliest times, with the ancient Coptic and Egyptian names.

The constellation drawings are from Bullinger's works which in turn are based on Jamieson's "Celestial Atlas" - 1820; Flammarion's "L'Etoiles"; Sir John W. Lubbock's "Stars in Six Maps" - 1883; and Edward J. Copper's "Egyptian Scenery" - 1820. Other sources used are: "Dawn of Astronomy" by J. Norman Lockyer - 1897; "Astronomy with the Naked Eye" by Garrett P. Serviss - 1909; "Encyclopedia Britannica" - 1943; "Splendor in the Sky" by Gerald S. Hawkins - 1961; "Introduction to Astronomy" by Charles M. Huffer, Frederick E. Trinklein, Mark Bunge - 1967.